# Simple Suggestions

## to Nourish the Mind, Body, and Spirit

### Elizabeth Baldwin-Lodge

*Very barely famous actress, award-winning interior designer, and family-proclaimed fabulous home chef*

**BALBOA**
PRESS

A DIVISION OF HAY HOUSE

Interior Graphics/Art Credit: Image by New Ground Photography

Balboa Press books may be ordered through booksellers or by contacting:

Balboa Press
A Division of Hay House
1663 Liberty Drive
Bloomington, IN 47403
www.balboapress.com
1 (877) 407-4847

Because of the dynamic nature of the Internet, any web addresses or links contained in this book may have changed since publication and may no longer be valid. The views expressed in this work are solely those of the author and do not necessarily reflect the views of the publisher, and the publisher hereby disclaims any responsibility for them.

The author of this book does not dispense medical advice or prescribe the use of any technique as a form of treatment for physical, emotional, or medical problems without the advice of a physician, either directly or indirectly. The intent of the author is only to offer information of a general nature to help you in your quest for emotional and spiritual well-being. In the event you use any of the information in this book for yourself, which is your constitutional right, the author and the publisher assume no responsibility for your actions.

Any people depicted in stock imagery provided by Thinkstock are models, and such images are being used for illustrative purposes only.
Certain stock imagery © Thinkstock.

Print information available on the last page.

ISBN: 978-1-5043-7068-4 (sc)
ISBN: 978-1-5043-7069-1 (hc)
ISBN: 978-1-5043-7075-2 (e)

Library of Congress Control Number: 2016919753

Balboa Press rev. date: 12/23/2016

Dedicated to everyone on the planet—

especially

Alexandra and John-Henry

To thine own self be true, and it must follow, as the night the day, thou canst not then be false to any man.
—William Shakespeare

The power of thought is one of the most primal force functions of all human beings. Without it, there is no way we could experience life.
—Sydney Banks

To laugh often and much; to win the respect of intelligent people and the affection of children; to earn the appreciation of honest critics and endure the betrayal of false friends; to appreciate beauty, to find the best in others; to leave the world a little better; whether by a healthy child, a garden patch or a redeemed social condition; to know even one life has breathed easier because you have lived. This is the meaning of success.
—Ralph Waldo Emerson

# Introduction

John Lennon said, "When I was five years old, my mother always told me that happiness was the key to life. When I went to school, they asked me what I wanted to be when I grew up. I wrote down 'happy'. They told me I didn't understand the assignment, and I told them they didn't understand life."

Feeling happy has been a lifelong quest for me. I have worn many hats during my endeavor of trying to figure out how to be happy. I am an actress, interior designer, inspirational motivator, and now a writer by profession. I am a mother, wife, daughter, and sister in life. I love to philosophize, travel, read historical fiction, cook and create recipes, watch films, go boating, be in nature, and have candlelit dinners. All of my roles, all of my creative pursuits, and all of my enjoyments have been an effort to fill a happiness void.

As a child, I wanted to be a movie star and thought that would make me happy. I moved to Malibu, California, to attend Pepperdine University to be close to Hollywood. However, after graduating with a degree in theater arts/communication and design, I moved to New York City to pursue my acting career. I was hired doing bit parts on soap operas and in films and felt good some of the time. Why not all the time, though? That was the question.

New York City is where I met my first husband, one of the famous Baldwin brothers. We both eventually moved back to Los Angeles, and that's where we got married and briefly worked on a sitcom together called *Sydney* with Valerie Bertinelli. This was thrilling as she was married to Eddie Van Halen at the time, and Van Halen was one of my favorite rock bands when I was growing up. Wow, it would appear I had it all. I was working as an actress, married to a celebrity, and meeting famous musicians and movie stars.

I enjoyed my work as an actress, but the marriage didn't fill my happiness void, and it ended for various reasons. I continued working as an actress in Los Angeles, again on soap operas, sitcoms, and films. I felt lonely, though, and craved being in a loving relationship. I met my second husband at a celebrity cricket match. So I next married into a famous musical family, the Moody Blues. Again, after many years of trying to fix the marriage, we ended up apart. It hadn't filled my happiness void. *What's wrong with me?* I thought. Once again, on the surface it would appear I had everything. *Why don't I feel happy inside?* I knew we humans must have fulfilling relationships to be truly happy. I read every relationship book I could find. I was always the first to tell my partner what he or we should be doing to improve our relationship so that we could be happy.

Then *flash*—I realized after attending a spiritual conference about how our thoughts create our reality that I had to live an inside-out life. Happiness comes from inside me, not anything outside of me. It comes from my relationship with myself. It doesn't come from my way of earning an income, although I enjoy my work. It doesn't come from an outside force, my partners, friends, family, children, or material possessions—although all of these can bring so much happiness. We have to be happy from the inside first to truly enjoy the outside things. But how do we accomplish being happy on the inside first?

Happiness is created by our thoughts, which create our emotions, which then create our reality. I put this insight to the test by stopping to notice what I was thinking about every time I wasn't feeling good.

My thoughts when I was feeling down were never happy, positive ones, and I finally realized, *yes, my thoughts are creating my suffering.* If I could change my thoughts, then I could change how I am feeling in any moment. Could it be that simple?

Sometimes it was that easy, and sometimes it was hard, especially if I was stuck in an old emotional pattern, constantly replaying the events of the past that had caused me so much pain, over and over in my mind. How could I stop doing this? I realized that doing the simple suggestions listed in this book took my mind off my negative thoughts. Gradually my mind would slide back to positive thoughts, and I would begin to feel happier.

So I wanted to share my simple suggestions. Realize that what you are thinking is creating your state of well- or ill-being. When you get stuck, move your thoughts back to positive, healthy ones by giving yourself knowledge, sustenance, and inspiration. These three key factors moved my thoughts back onto a track of happiness when I was stuck in a negative habitual thinking pattern.

I hope it will do the same for you.

My *Simple Suggestions* inspirations came to me as follows:

Flash No. 1—My son came home from school one day and said, "Mom, I know what negative two minus negative two is." He was so proud of this knowledge and even more proud that he was the only one in his class who solved the problem. He was feeling enormous joy and self-satisfaction.

It feels really good to learn. Learning stimulates our thought processes, which in turn creates a self-satisfying emotional state. Knowledge building makes us happy, so learn something new as often as possible.

Flash No. 2—I realized I looked forward to at least one yummy meal a day. I found myself thinking about whatever delicious meal I wanted to prepare. Thinking about it gave me a satiating feeling. It may be a very healthy meal, or it may be a comforting meal. If eating completely healthy makes you feel good, choose one of the Paleo or gluten-free recipes. If you want a comforting meal, choose one of those recipes. Balance in all things is the key for me. Good food is for building our bodies' energies; it feels great to fuel our bodies. Food makes me happy.

Flash No. 3—It's a wonderful feeling to read or hear words of inspiration. Inspirational quotes stimulated my thoughts. They guided me to view life more positively. Happy thoughts create joyful feelings and bring more peace and calm into our lives.

Flash No. 4—Being kind and doing something for myself or others lifted my spirit beyond measure. Kindness creates an emotional warmth that releases a hormone known as oxytocin. Oxytocin helps reduce blood pressure, lowers anxiety, and gives us an overall feeling of bliss.

I hope everyone reading *Simple Suggestions to Nourish the Mind, Body, and Spirit* realizes in a *flash* what took me a long time to understand. My only intention for writing *Simple Suggestions* is that it may bring you more peace, tranquility, and joy to your life. There are no instructions, except you may want to carry it with you as a reminder to guide yourself back to bliss whenever and as often as you need; also, it's a convenient way to have the recipes with you when you're at the supermarket.

The order of the pages is not important. Open the book randomly and see which page you land on.

The mind section offers a question to enhance your knowledge. The body section offers delicious recipes. There is a variety, from

Paleo to gluten-free and everything in between. They have been compiled from old family recipes and trial and error of what I found delicious—I hope you do too. The spirit section offers an uplifting quote as well as a suggested activity to nourish yourself or others. Several of my favorite activities are listed twice. The answers to the mind questions are in the back of the book as well as all of the suggested spirit activities.

Lastly, pass *Simple Suggestions* forward to someone you know who may need some fun suggestions to move through his or her stuck thought patterns and live a more fulfilling, happy life.

# Acknowledgments

With so much gratitude, I wish to thank the teachings of the following people:

Louise L. Hay, Dr. Wayne Dyer, Esther and Jerry Hicks—the Abraham teachings, Edgar Cayce, Reverend Sally Perry, Jane Roberts and Robert Butts—the teachings of Seth, Sonia Choquette, Shatki Gawain, Rhonda Byrne, Sarah Ban Breathnach, Dr. Brian Weiss, Julia Cameron, Dan Millman, Richard Bach, Dr. Mary Lou Rane, Sandy Brewer, Dr. Deepak Chopra, Marianne Williamson, Neal Donald Walsch, Anna Raimondi, Michael Beckwith, Eckhart Tolle, Sydney Banks, George and Linda Pranksy, Michael Neill, and Elsie Spittle.

They all have inspired me to live a blessed and very grateful life.

# Mind No. 1

Which planet is naturally the brightest object in the night sky?

# Body

## Thai-Inspired Meatballs
Serves 4 (Paleo and gluten free)

1 1/2 pounds ground turkey or chicken
1 carrot
1 celery stalk
2 garlic cloves
1/2 cup shredded coconut
1 egg
2 teaspoons curry powder
1/2 teaspoon salt
pinch of cayenne pepper
handful of cilantro

Chop or food process all ingredients—except the meat choice—until fine.

Add the meat to the chopped ingredients and make as many meatballs as desired. The larger the ball, the longer it takes them to cook.

Heat some oil in a large pan over medium to medium-high heat. Drop the meatballs in when the oil is hot enough to instantly sizzle.

Cook the meatballs for several minutes on each side; then cover and cook for 8 to 10 minutes more.

## Spirit

We are shaped by our thoughts; we become what we think. When the mind is pure, joy follows like a shadow that never leaves. —Buddha

## *Walk

Take a thirty-minute walk. I'm so grateful to live close to the beach; this is my Zen walking space.

Wherever you live, find a path as close to nature as possible for your walk. Listen to the sound of the waves, hear the birds sing, feel the breeze, listen to the waterfall, smell the pine trees, breathe in the beauty, and still your thoughts to your immediate surroundings.

Walking clears my self-talk and allows thoughtful insights of the universe to come forward. Some of my greatest inspirations have come forth when I've been on a walk.

# Mind No. 2

How many times a year does the sun rise and set at the North Pole?

## Body

### Creamy Dreamy Tomato Soup
Serves 6 (gluten-free- if you leave out the croutons.)

2 tablespoons butter
2 tablespoons olive oil
1 onion, finely chopped
2 pounds' tomatoes, chopped
2 3/4 cups vegetable stock
1/2 cup dry white wine
2 tablespoons tomato paste
sea salt to taste
pinch of cayenne pepper
2 tablespoons chopped fresh basil leaves
2/3 cup heavy cream
fresh basil leaves or croutons to garnish (optional)

In a big, sturdy pan, combine the butter and oil, and melt. Add the onion, and sauté until the onion is soft, 3 to 5 minutes. Add the rest of the ingredients and stir. Add sea salt and cayenne pepper to taste.

Leave the lid slightly ajar and simmer for 20 to 25 minutes. Stir occasionally until the ingredients have a soft texture.

Take the pan off the heat and let the mixture cool down for 5 minutes. Transfer to a blender, add the basil, and blend. Strain the soup through a colander into a new pan, add the cream, and warm the soup. Do not boil.

Add a basil leaf for garnish and serve.

# Spirit

Whether you think you can or whether you think you can't, you're right.
—Henry Ford

# * Meditate

I like to light a fragrant candle before I begin my meditation, as it relaxes and centers me before beginning. I love listening to *Getting into the Vortex*, fifteen-minute guided meditations from Esther and Jerry Hicks (Abraham). There are so many great guided meditations available. I also love Dr. Brian Weiss's guided healing meditations, Wayne Dyer's *ah* and *om* meditations, and Sonia Choquette's guided meditations, or I simply sit quietly and focus on good-feeling thoughts and positive intentions for five minutes. Morning is a great time for meditation, as it sets forth a powerful course for your day.

# Mind No. 3

What was the world's first electrically lighted city?

## Body

### Melon, Prosciutto, Ham, and Parmesan Salad
Serves 4 (gluten-free)

1/5 of a watermelon (about 2 pounds), peeled, seeded, and thinly sliced
2/3 of a honeydew melon (about 2 pounds), peeled, seeded, and thinly sliced
1 large cantaloupe (about 2 pounds), peeled, seeded, and thinly sliced
5 ounces sliced prosciutto ham
1 ounce Parmesan cheese, finely shaved
1 cup fresh basil

Dressing:
1/4 cup light olive oil
1/4 cup aged sherry vinegar
salt and pepper to taste

Arrange the watermelon, honeydew, and cantaloupe slices on a large serving plate.

I like to alternate the three melons to be decorative. Wrap the prosciutto around or drape it over the melon slices.

For the dressing, combine the olive oil and sherry vinegar in a container with a tight lid, add salt and pepper to taste, and shake well.

Gently pour the dressing over the melon and ham. Place the shaved Parmesan and basil over the dressing.

Best served immediately.

# Spirit

Your only obligation in any lifetime is to be true to yourself.
—Richard Bach

# * Massage

Treat yourself to a massage. Some studies have found that massage may be beneficial for anxiety, digestive disorders, fibromyalgia, headaches, insomnia-related stress, soft tissue strains or injuries, and sports injuries. Massages are now so affordable, with options like Hand and Stone Spa and Massage Envy club memberships. I treat myself to a massage at least once a month, and you should too.

# Mind No. 4

What institution awards the Pulitzer Prize?

# Body

## Breakfast Burritos
Serves 2

2 flour tortillas (10 inch–12 inch work best, can use gluten free tortillas)
3–4 eggs
2 slices of bacon
1 large sausage (can be any meat, precooked)
1/2 medium onion, chopped
1 small parboiled potato, cubed
1 jalapeño pepper, seeded and chopped fine (optional)
1/2 cup shredded cheddar cheese (or cheese of your choice)
salt and pepper to taste
picante sauce or salsa

Cut the bacon slices into pieces and cook. Add sausage when bacon is halfway done.

Add potato and sauté about 3 to 5 minutes.

Add onion and jalapeño pepper, and sauté 2 to 3 more minutes. (Bacon fat doesn't need to be drained unless desired.)

In a separate bowl, scramble the eggs. Pour scrambled eggs into the skillet and cook. Add cheese just before the eggs reach the desired consistency.

Heat tortillas slightly. (I use the microwave.) Spoon egg mixture onto tortilla and roll into burrito.

Serve with picante sauce or salsa on top.

## Spirit

Holding onto anger is like drinking poison and expecting the other person to die.
—Buddha

## * Read a Book

Take the time to browse through a bookstore. I love to get a coffee or green tea and roam. I can spend a good hour choosing my next adventure. Reading, for me, has always been a favorite gift to myself. I love historical fiction because it's educational and exciting. I also like to read at least one chapter of an inspirational book every morning. I was given *Illusions* by Richard Bach when I was eighteen, and it set my life on a course for which I'm forever grateful. Look at the acknowledgments page of this book for the names of authors of inspirational books. They're all brilliant. A chapter a day keeps the blues away. It always sets such a happy course for my day.

# Mind No. 5

What is the strongest bone in the body?

## Body

### Broccoli or Cauliflower with Herbs
Serves 4 (Paleo and gluten free)

1 1/2 pounds broccoli or cauliflower (or mix them)
3 tablespoons extra virgin olive oil
3 large garlic cloves, chopped fine
1/2–1 teaspoon of crushed red pepper flakes
2 tablespoons of Italian herbs (dried or fresh)
4 tablespoons butter
1/4 cup fresh chives chopped
1 ounce Parmesan cheese, shaved
sea salt and pepper to taste

Trim the broccoli or cauliflower and cut to desired length and size. Steam gently for no more than 2 minutes, and immediately remove from heat; set aside. Save a little bit of the broccoli water. Over medium to low heat, add oil and sauté garlic for 2–3 minutes, until slightly brown. Adjust the heat to medium, and add the broccoli and 3–4 tablespoons of the broccoli cooking water. Season with the red pepper flakes, Italian herbs, salt, and pepper. Sauté for 4–6 minutes more or until the broccoli is barely tender. Add butter and toss the broccoli. Remove from heat and put on serving dish. Sprinkle the cheese and chives over the broccoli.

# Spirit

We must develop and maintain the capacity to forgive. He who is devoid of the power to forgive is devoid of the power to love. There is some good in the worst of us and some evil in the best of us.
—Martin Luther King Jr.

# * Dream Board

Create a dream board. Cut out pictures from magazines or print pictures from the Internet, and paste them on a white poster board. They could be pictures of things you would like to have, places you'd like to visit, a car you'd like to drive, a beautiful bouquet of flowers, the perfect job, jewelry you'd like, a relationship you'd like to be in, or your dream house. Fill your board with anything that you would love to have, be, or experience. I keep mine close to my desk, and every time I glance at it, a feeling of grateful expectation fills my being.

# Mind No. 6

What is the body's strongest substance?

## Body

Seriously Scrumptious Split-Pea Soup
Serves 4 (gluten free)

3 cloves garlic, minced
1 onion, chopped
1 tablespoon olive oil
1 tablespoon butter
salt and pepper
2 tablespoons dried Italian herbs
8 cups (2 quarts) chicken stock
1 pound dried split peas, rinsed
2 carrots, diced
2 celery stalks, diced
1 1/2 cups ham or pancetta, cubed
1/4 cup chopped parsley

Heat the butter and olive oil in a large saucepan. Add the onions, and sauté until softened; then put in the garlic, Italian seasonings, salt, and pepper. Continue to sauté for several more minutes. Pour in the chicken stock and split peas. Once it reaches boiling, reduce heat and let simmer, covered, for 1 hour. Add the carrots, celery, cubed ham or pancetta, and parsley. Gently simmer uncovered for 30 minutes. Add more seasoning to taste.

## Spirit

If you are depressed, you are living in the past. If you are anxious you are living in the future. If you are at peace you are living in the present.
—Lao Tzu

## * Make Amends

Forgiveness is one of the most beneficial gifts you can give yourself. So make amends with anyone, you feel negativity towards, regardless of whether you are actually able to speak with the person or not. If you are unable to have a conversation, another excellent way to accomplish forgiveness is to write forgiving statements. In your journal or on a piece of paper, just write it out. It can be as simple as writing, "[insert name,] I forgive you for all the things that have made me feel hurt, sad, or rejected. I also forgive myself for all the parts I have played in our relationship." I have found that repeatedly writing out the sentence, until I feel all negative feelings are released, is the best way to cleanse pent-up emotions and clear out old thought patterns.

# Mind No. 7

In what year did the construction of the Berlin Wall begin?

## Body

Garlicky Mashed Potatoes
Serves 4–6 (gluten free)

2 large or 3 medium russet potatoes
4 cloves of garlic chopped fine
2 tablespoons of olive oil
1/2 cup half-and-half
4 tablespoons of butter
salt to taste

Peel, cut, and boil potatoes (test with fork for doneness).

Sauté garlic in olive oil for 2–3 minutes; set aside.

Drain potatoes. Add garlic, half-and-half, butter, and salt. Mix with electric beater until whipped.

## Spirit

Security is mostly a superstition. It does not exist in nature, nor do the children of men as a whole experience it. Avoiding danger is no

safer in the long run than outright exposure. Life is either a daring adventure, or nothing.
—Helen Keller

## * Yoga

Take a yoga class; it's so good for your body. Yoga lowers stress and improves your mood. Some yoga methods use specific meditation techniques to focus the mind on your breathing, which quiets the constant "mind chatter," allowing you to feel relaxed. Yoga also can boost oxygen levels to the brain, leaving you feeling happy and more content with everyday life.

# Mind No. 8

What is the only number with the same number of letters as the meaning of its name?

## Body

Festive Fajitas
Serves 4

1 tablespoon olive oil
2 large sweet onions, thinly sliced
1 red bell pepper, cut into thin strips
1 yellow or orange pepper cut into thin strips (Can use a green pepper; I prefer the others.)
2 teaspoons fresh or dried Italian herbs
1 one-pound beef flank or sirloin steak
1 cup grated cheddar cheese (optional)
sea salt and cracked black pepper to taste
4 eight-inch tortillas, warmed up (can use gluten free tortillas)

In a large pan, heat the olive oil over medium-high heat. Reduce the heat to medium-low, add the onions, and cover. Sauté until tender, about 10 minutes.

Uncover and add the bell peppers and Italian herbs; sauté for 4 to 5 minutes more.

When the onions are golden and the peppers are al dente, remove from heat.

Trim fat from the steak, if desired. (I keep the fat on for added flavor.) Season with desired spices.

Start outdoor barbecue grill. When the barbecue is at medium-high heat, grill the steak for 8–12 minutes, turning once for medium-rare. (Alternately, steak can be cooked inside under broiler or in skillet.)

Slice the steak diagonally across the grain in desired thickness. Place the steak slices in warm tortillas, and top with the onion mixture and cheese. Roll them up to serve.

## Spirit

Try not to become a person of success, but rather try to become a person of value.
—Albert Einstein

## * Ring, Ring

If you find yourself thinking about an old friend, make that connection; reach out to him or her. I lost one of my closet college friends to cancer at age forty-seven. I had not seen her for over ten years and kept thinking about connecting with her. Unexpectedly, I was able to visit her on a trip to Washington, DC, a few months before her diagnosis. I am forever grateful I made the time to visit and see her happy and full of life. Follow your intuition when a friend or relative pops into your head. Reach out to him or her in the moment.

# Mind No. 9

How many people signed the Declaration of Independence?

# Body

## Muma's Oatmeal Muffins
Serves 24 (one muffin each)

1 1/2 cups bran cereal (any kind)
1 1/2 cups old-fashioned uncooked oatmeal
1 cup boiling water
1/2 cup butter
1/2 quart buttermilk
1 1/2 cups sugar
2 eggs
2 1/2 cups flour (can be sifted)
2 1/2 teaspoons baking soda
1/2 teaspoons salt
1/2 teaspoons cinnamon
1 cup raisins (optional)

Place 1 cup of bran cereal and 1 cup boiling water in a bowl. Set aside.

In large mixing bowl, cream butter, sugar, and eggs.

Add buttermilk and soaked bran mixture. Add flour, baking soda, and salt. When flour is dampened, add oatmeal and remaining 1/2 cup of dry bran cereal. Add cinnamon and raisins.

Spray muffin tins with cooking spray oil, and spoon mixture into tins.

Bake for 20 minutes at 375 degrees on middle rack.

Muffins are done when a toothpick inserted in the middle comes out clean. Let cool.

# Spirit

Be in a state of gratitude for everything that shows up in your life. Be thankful for the storms as well as smooth sailing.
—Dr. Wayne Dyer

# * Spring Clean

Clean out your closet. It doesn't have to be spring—let it be summer, fall, or winter as well. When we clear out the old, it makes room for the new. I know it's cliché, but it's true. I love shopping, so clearing out leaves room to fill the hole I just created. This is a double-sided gift. Give your gently worn items to someone who has a hole in his or her closet. It could be a friend, coworker, employee, the Red Cross, Goodwill, the Salvation Army, or anyone in need. I have a few friends whose "gently worn" clothes I would love to have. You could also sell them or consign them and earn a little money—, that always makes me happy.

# Mind No. 10

What is the most common element in the universe?

# Body

Queen Elizabeth's Shepherd's Pie
Serves 6–8

2 pounds lean ground beef
3 tablespoons olive oil
1 1/2 large onion, chopped
3–4 cloves garlic, chopped
2 cups carrots, chopped
2 pounds peeled and cut potatoes for mashing (For a Paleo option, use 2 pounds of cauliflower instead of potatoes.)
3 Oxo cubes (beef bouillon)
4–5 tablespoons Worcestershire sauce
1/2 bottle beer (optional; use one cup of beef broth as substitute)
3 tablespoons heavy cream
6 tablespoons butter
1 cup whole milk
1 cup of grated cheddar cheese
½ teaspoon of salt, pepper, and seasoning salt or more to taste

In a large iron skillet, heat the olive oil on medium-high. Add onion, garlic, salt, pepper, and seasoning salt. Sauté until golden.

Add ground beef. Crumble 3 Oxo cubes onto meat. Add Worcestershire sauce, beer, and heavy cream. Stir until meat is browned. Do not drain.

Add carrots. (Add another Oxo cube and a 1/2 cup of water or beef broth to cook the carrots.) Reduce heat to medium-low; cover with lid or aluminum foil. Cook for 50 minutes.

Bring water to boil in large pot. Add potatoes; cook until tender to mash. Drain potatoes; return to pot. Add 4 tablespoons of butter, milk, and salt to taste. Mash.

Compact meat in skillet by pressing down with spatula.
Spread mashed potatoes over meat. Melt the remaining two tablespoons of butter and pour evenly over potatoes, sprinkle with cheese. Place skillet under broiler until cheese bubbles golden brown.

# Spirit

Iron rusts from disuse; stagnant water loses it purity and in cold weather becomes frozen; even so does inaction sap the vigor of the mind.
—Leonardo da Vinci

# * Grateful Eight

Make a list of eight things for which you are grateful. It could be anything. For example,

- I'm grateful that I was on time for work today.
- I'm grateful there was no traffic on my way to work.
- I'm grateful for my car, as it is my sanctuary where I listen to music while I travel.

- I'm grateful for my house. It brings me a sense of peace and safety every time I enter it.
- I'm grateful for my health and want to thank each cell in my body for doing its job seemingly effortlessly.
- I'm so grateful for my friends and family. They are always there to listen to me and lend me support.
- I'm grateful for being able to travel. It exhilarates my soul.
- I'm grateful for my spouse. His or her smile always brightens my day.

You get the idea. Be sure to write the reasons why you are grateful. Writing the reasons will boost your vibration even higher, and you will feel gratitude more deeply.

# Mind No. 11

At which temperature do Celsius and Fahrenheit meet?

# Body

### Devilish Deviled Eggs
Serves 6-8 (Paleo and gluten free)

12 large hard-boiled eggs, peeled and cut in half
3–4 tablespoons mayonnaise
1 small celery stalk, chopped fine
1 teaspoon of yellow or Dijon mustard
Pinch of smoked paprika
Pinch of garlic powder
Sea salt and pinch of cayenne pepper to taste
4 teaspoons chopped chives to garnish

Boil the eggs for 12 minutes. Carefully drain the hot water and fill pan with cold water. Let eggs cool down. Gently peel and cut in half.

Remove the yolks and place in a small bowl. Add the mayonnaise, celery, mustard, paprika, and garlic powder, and mash until smooth. Season to taste with salt and pepper.

Spoon the yolk mixture back into the egg whites.

Sprinkle with the chives. Refrigerate until ready to serve.

# Spirit

Only those who will risk going too far can possibly find out how far one can go.

—T. S. Elliot

## * Mirror, Mirror on the Wall

Look in the mirror and tell yourself how loved and appreciated you are, at least eight times out loud or until you really mean it. Yes, it can feel awkward at first, but it's a great exercise. I learned this exercise from Louise Hay. She offers so many self-love activities. Explore more at Hayhouse.com. It all begins with the love of ourselves.

# Mind No. 12

Which novel does Nick Carraway narrate?

# Body

Savory Shrimp Quesadillas
Serves 2

2 teaspoons olive oil
1 clove garlic, chopped
6–8 raw shrimp, peeled and deveined
1/2 cup red onion, chopped
1/2 red bell pepper, chopped
1 cup fresh spinach, chopped
1/4 cup Worcestershire sauce
2 tortillas (can use gluten free)
1/2 cup shredded cheddar cheese (or cheese of choice)
1/4 cup cilantro
cooking spray (such as Pam)
salsa and sour cream (optional)

Heat oil in a nonstick skillet. Add garlic and shrimp, and cook for 1–2 minutes per side, until shrimp is pink.

Add vegetables and Worcestershire sauce. Cook for an additional 5 minutes; remove to bowl.

Spray the skillet with cooking spray; place tortilla in pan, and top half the tortilla with shrimp mixture and cheese. Fold tortilla in half and cook for 2 minutes per side, pressing down with spatula until cheese melts.

Serve topped with salsa and sour cream.

## Spirit

There is no such thing as an absolutely right decision or wrong decision. We make our decisions to move forward with the best understanding we have at the time.
—Deepak Chopra

## *Facial

Give your face a present and have a facial. Facial treatments feel good, offering soothing relaxation. They increase circulation and blood flow, relieve stress, and encourage peace of mind and contentment. A good facial (and facial massage) can help smooth fine lines and promote collagen production, which is the building block of the skin, to prevent premature aging, wrinkles, and sagging. Facials are fabulous.

# Mind No. 13

What country has the world's longest coastline?

# Body

### Steak or Lamb Shish Kabobs
Serves 4 (Paleo and gluten free)

1 pound of sirloin or boneless lamb loin, trimmed of fat and cut into 1-inch cubes
2 tablespoons of olive oil, plus a little extra to drizzle over kabobs before cooking
1/4 cup red wine
1 small onion, finely chopped
1–2 garlic cloves, crushed
2 tablespoons dried Italian herbs
1 medium red onion, cut into six wedges and separated
1 medium red pepper, deseeded, cut into 1-inch pieces
1 medium green pepper, deseeded, cut into 1-inch pieces
16 large cherry tomatoes

Use metal skewers (or soak wood ones to prevent charring). Combine olive oil, chopped onion, garlic, red wine, and Italian herbs in bowl. Add meat, and marinate for one hour. On a grill, heat to medium-high. Skewer marinated meat, alternating with onion, peppers, and tomatoes. Salt and pepper to taste. Sprinkle extra olive oil over kabobs, and grill for 2–3 minutes each side, or longer for more well-done meat.

# Spirit

I have always been delighted at the prospect of a new day, a fresh try, one more start, with perhaps a bit of magic waiting somewhere behind the morning.
—J. B. Priestley

# *Stay-cation

Occasionally, I like to just stay home and do nothing. I like to use the term *stay-cation* because it's a vacation while staying home. Whatever your *nothing* is, do that while on your stay-cation—binge-watch a TV series, bake a cake, or lie in bed all day. Invite friends to stay for the weekend and lounge around, playing games and laughing.

# Mind No. 14

What is the earth's circumference in miles?

# Body

## Day-Dreamy Creamy Mushroom Soup
Serves 8 (one cup each) gluten free

1 tablespoon butter
1 clove garlic
1 medium white onion, chopped
1 teaspoon celery salt
1 pound mushrooms (white and portobello), chopped
1 cup water
1 cup whole milk
2 cups chicken broth
2 tablespoons dried Italian herbs
3 tablespoons red wine or brandy
1/4 cup heavy whipping cream
croutons (optional)

Melt the butter gradually in pan. Sauté the garlic and onion in butter over medium heat. Reduce heat to low, and cook for 5 minutes, stirring frequently. Slowly add mushrooms, celery salt, and Italian seasonings. Cook for 5 more minutes.

Add water, milk, broth, wine, and cream. Simmer for 20 minutes.

Pour into a blender or food processor, and blend on low until creamy and smooth.

Serve warm. Garnish with croutons, if desired.

# Spirit

Twenty years from now you will be more disappointed by the things that you didn't do than by the ones you did do. So throw off the bowlines. Sail away from the safe harbor. Catch the trade winds in your sails. Explore. Dream. Discover.
—Mark Twain

# * Rock and Roll

I had forgotten how awesome it is to attend a concert. What an extraordinary sensation it is to hear live music you love. I recently saw U2, one of my all-time favorite bands. I had not seen them in a decade and was walking on cloud nine for days. So many of their songs bring back fabulous memories and good-feeling thoughts.

# Mind No. 15

Which volcanic eruption destroyed the Roman cities of Pompeii and Herculaneum?

## Body

### Prosciutto-Wrapped Chicken with Spinach and Feta
Serves 4 (Paleo and gluten free)

1 tablespoon butter
2 teaspoons olive oil, plus extra for brushing
4 boneless, skinless chicken breasts
garlic salt
freshly ground black pepper
2 garlic cloves, finely chopped
1/3 cup feta cheese
1/3 cup grated Parmesan cheese
2 tablespoons chopped flat-leaf (Italian) parsley
2 cups fresh chopped spinach
8 thin prosciutto slices

Lightly grease a baking sheet. Preheat oven to 350 degrees F. Heat butter and oil in a large skillet over high heat. Season chicken with garlic salt and pepper, and brown quickly on both sides. Remove from pan to a plate.

Sauté garlic for two to three minutes. Cool a little. Combine feta, Parmesan, parsley, and garlic with chopped spinach.

Cut a pocket about 2 inches deep along the side of each chicken breast with a sharp knife. Fill each pocket with a quarter of the filling. Pinch meat over the filling to close the pocket.

Wrap chicken breast with prosciutto, brush with extra olive oil, and place on the baking sheet. Bake for 12–15 minutes or until cooked through. Allow chicken to rest for a few minutes before serving.

Serve whole or slice each breast on an angle.

# Spirit

How wonderful it is that nobody need wait a single moment before starting to improve the world.
—Anne Frank

# * Mani-Pedi

Schedule an appointment for a manicure and/or pedicure—you deserve it! I don't always have time for both, but I certainly make it a point to have one or the other. It is relaxing, calming, and refreshing. Invite a friend. Perhaps go for a meal afterward to celebrate your beautiful new nails. Guys, this is for you too. I know many men who love to get mani-pedis. If you haven't tried it, don't be afraid. Now is the time.

# Mind No. 16

Where in the body is blood produced?

# Body

## Charlie's Chopped Salad
Serves 4–5

8 ounces mixed greens
1 large Granny Smith apple, peeled and diced
1/2 cup walnut halves
1/4 red onion, sliced thin
1/2 large cucumber, sliced and halved
1/2 cup dried cranberries or cherries, or mix of both
6 ounces bleu cheese or Roquefort, crumbled
8 slices thick-cut bacon, cooked

Dressing
3 tablespoons apple cider vinegar
2 tablespoons orange juice
2 1/2 teaspoons Dijon mustard
2 tablespoons honey or agave syrup
1 teaspoon sea salt
2/3 cup olive oil
sea salt and fresh ground pepper to taste

In large bowl combine mixed greens, apple, walnuts, red onion, cucumber, cranberries/cherries, and bleu cheese. Chop the bacon into large pieces, and add it to the salad.

Whisk together the vinegar, orange juice, mustard, honey, and 1 teaspoon sea salt. Gradually whisk in olive oil. Toss lightly with the salad. Add fresh ground pepper to taste.

## Spirit

Worrying is using your imagination to create something you don't want.
—Esther and Jerry Hicks (Abraham)

# * Pay That Toll

Surprise the car behind you on the toll way by paying its toll. It may be a blessing in disguise. A friend of mine lost her father unexpectedly and was grieving. She was asking for a sign that her father was still near and that he knew how much she loved him. She received her sign while driving through a toll booth. As she handed her fare to the toll booth operator, he said, "The car in front already paid for you." It was the same random act of kindness her father always did. She knew then that her father was close and that all was well. It comforted her greatly.

# Mind No. 17

What is a group of owls called?

# Body

## Ooey-Gooey Chicken Legs
Serves 4 (gluten free)

8–10 large chicken legs

Marinade
2 garlic cloves, minced
1/4 cup vegetable or coconut oil
1 tablespoon grated fresh ginger (or powdered)
finely grated zest and juice of 1 lime or lemon
1 tablespoon honey or light brown sugar
1 tablespoon Worcestershire sauce
1 tablespoon sweet chili sauce
2 tablespoons tomato ketchup
1 tablespoon vinegar
2 teaspoons ground cumin

Heat grill to medium or preheat oven to 350 degrees F. If using oven, spray cooking oil in swallow baking pan. Mix the ingredients for marinade in a bowl. Toss the chicken in the marinade; then refrigerator for 1–2 hours, covered.

Thirty minutes before cooking, take chicken legs out of fridge.

Remove chicken legs from marinade, and place the legs in the baking pan or on the grill.

Reserve marinade to pour over legs during cooking. Bake/grill for 35–45 minutes or until cooked through.

# Spirit

The state of your life is nothing more than a reflection of your state of mind.
—Dr. Wayne Dyer

# * Join That Gym

Join that gym you keep talking about; just do it! Keeping your body healthy and strong is an anti-stress agent. Most gyms are very affordable now and offer a complimentary training session to help you get started. Gyms also offer great classes, such as spinning, yoga, boot camp, and Zumba. If weights are not your thing, there are so many other options at the gym now. You will be pleasantly surprised by how much more energy you will have. Dopamine, a neurotransmitter in the brain, is released when we exercise. Dopamine is necessary for feelings of pleasure and happiness. The more we work out, the happier we are.

# Mind No. 18

How many years did Nelson Mandela spend in prison before his release in 1990?

# Body

## Leaning Tower of Pizza
Serves 4–6

2 precooked Italian sausages, sliced
4 ounces pepperoni slices (I use Applegate Naturals turkey pepperoni.)
1 cup fresh mushrooms, sliced
1 fresh tomato, chopped
1/4 cup fresh basil, finely chopped
1 teaspoon dried Italian herbs
1–2 cups shredded mozzarella
1/2–1 cup tomato sauce or marinara sauce (can use pasta sauce)
2 large tortillas (can use gluten free tortillas)
(Use your choice of toppings; those listed are my favorites.)
Parmesan and crushed red chilies (optional)

Place tortillas on baking sheet. Spread tomato sauce evenly over tortillas. Place shredded mozzarella evenly over tortillas. Place sausage and pepperoni slices evenly around tortillas. Place sliced mushrooms and tomato evenly around tortillas. Sprinkle herbs and basil over tortillas evenly.

Place on baking sheet, and bake on center rack at 375 degrees for 10–15 minutes. Remove, and place on cutting board. Slice into pieces. Sprinkle with Parmesan and crushed red chilies (optional).

# Spirit

It is one of the most beautiful compensations of this life that no man can sincerely try to help another without helping himself. ... Serve and thou shall be served.
—Ralph Waldo Emerson

# * Theater or Comedy

Go see a theatrical production or a comedy show. It doesn't have to be Broadway or the West End. Most cities and towns have local theater—attend! If comedy is your thing, go to a comedy club, and laugh, laugh, laugh. Either experience is vitalizing.

# Mind No. 19

Which city had the world's first paved streets?

# Body

Come On, Baby—Let's Tuna Twist
Serves 4 (gluten free)

4–6 baby carrots, finely chopped
1 stalk celery, finely chopped
2 cloves garlic, finely chopped
1 small onion, finely chopped
1/2 cup chopped cilantro
1/2 cup drained garbanzo beans or black beans (optional)
2 12-ounce cans tuna
1/2 cup mayonnaise
1 tablespoon Dijon mustard
1 teaspoon garlic powder
salt, pepper, and Italian seasonings to taste
mixed greens

Chop the carrots, celery, garlic, onion, and cilantro. Place in a bowl and save.

In another bowl, mix the tuna, mayonnaise, mustard, garlic powder, salt, pepper, Italian seasonings, and beans (if desired).

Add the vegetables to the tuna mixture and combine well. Add more seasonings to taste. Serve on a bed of mixed greens.

## Spirit

You may encounter many defeats, but you must not be defeated.
—Dr. Maya Angelou

## * Play

Go play tennis, golf, racquet ball, or soccer. Dance around your living room, or take a dance class. Learn to tango. Go outside and shoot hoops, kick a ball, or go for a bike ride. Be a kid again. Play and be *happy*.

# Mind No. 20

What is the fastest growing organ?

# Body

## Chicago Chicken in Wine Sauce
Serves 6

4 cups carrots
1 (approx. 4 1/2–5 pounds) chicken, cut into parts
salt, pepper, and Italian herbs to taste
1 tablespoon butter
1 medium onion, chopped
3 cloves garlic, minced
3 tablespoons flour
2 tablespoons tomato paste
1 1/2 cups red or white wine
1 cup of chicken broth
1 bay leaf
1 ounce fresh thyme
1 ounce fresh rosemary
1 1/2 cups small white mushrooms

Preheat the oven to 350 degrees. Steam carrots for 10 minutes. Set aside. Season the chicken with salt, pepper, thyme, rosemary, and Italian herbs. Add butter to an oven-safe dish, and sauté the chicken over medium to high heat for approximately 4–5 minutes on each side. Remove the chicken and set aside. In the same oven-safe dish, sauté the onion and garlic for 3–5 minutes until golden. Add the flour and tomato paste, reduce the heat to low, and cook a few more minutes until it forms a roux sauce. Add the wine, broth, bay leaf, thyme, and rosemary. Bring to a boil; then reduce the heat to low. Add the sautéed chicken to the wine broth. Cover and bake in oven for 10 minutes. Remove from the oven, and add the mushrooms and steamed carrots. Cover and bake 15 minutes more or until vegetables are desired doneness.

## Spirit

A man who is master of himself can end a sorrow as he can invent a pleasure. I don't want to be at the mercy of my emotions. I want to use them, to enjoy them, and to dominate them.
—Oscar Wilde

## * Be of Service

Donate your time. I have friends who rescue animals weekly from shelters. Serve a meal at a homeless shelter, even if it's a once-a-year Thanksgiving dinner. A dear friend of mine donates her time to prison inmates. She spends entire weekends in the prison, uplifting the inmates' spirits by sharing her loving wisdom and guiding them to see their self-worth. A remarkable way to be truly grateful for what we have, each and every day, is by giving to others.

# Mind No. 21

What does the acronym RADAR mean?

# Body

## Basic Baked Cod
Serves 4 (Paleo and gluten free)

1 1/2 pounds of wild-caught Alaska cod fillets (fresh or frozen)
1 1/2 tablespoons lemon juice
2 tablespoons olive oil
1/2 cup grated Parmesan cheese
sea salt, garlic salt, Italian seasoning, and black or cayenne pepper
to taste

Preheat oven to 375 degrees F. Spray baking pan with cooking oil.
Rinse fillets and pat dry. Place fillets in pan. Pour lemon juice oven
fillets evenly.

Drizzle olive oil over fillets evenly. Season with salts, Italian herbs,
and pepper. Sprinkle Parmesan cheese evenly over each fillet. Bake
for 12–15 minutes or until desired texture. May place under broiler
for last few minutes.

# Spirit

No matter what it is, if you really want it, and if you get out of the way of it, it will happen. It must be. It is Law. It can be no other way. It's the way this Universe is established. If you want it and you relax, it will happen.

—Esther and Jerry Hicks (Abraham)

# * Salt Bath

Take a hot twenty-minute mineral salt bath. I love to soak in Dr. Teal's Epsom salts. My favorite is the lavender or the eucalyptus. Not only do the minerals relax and sooth the body, but I get the benefits of aromatherapy too. Pleasant aromas release serotonin, which is the brain's natural happy chemical. I buy Dr. Teal's Epsom salts in my local supermarket, and they are quite affordable. This is a great gift to give yourself before bed. Lighting a candle while soaking brings even more relaxation.

# Mind No. 22

Marble is formed by the metamorphosis of what rock?

# Body

Cobb Salad with Chicken
Serves 4-6

Ranch Dressing
1–2 clove garlic
1/4 teaspoon sea salt
1 cup real mayonnaise
1/2 cup sour cream
1/4 cup Italian flat-leaf parsley leaves, minced
2 tablespoons fresh dill, minced
1 tablespoon minced fresh chives
1 teaspoon Worcestershire sauce
1/2 teaspoon ground black pepper
1/2 teaspoon white vinegar
1/4 teaspoon paprika
1/8 teaspoon cayenne pepper
Dash hot sauce (optional)
1/4 to 1/2 cup heavy cream, as needed

Cobb Salad
6 slices bacon

1 pound thin chicken breasts fillets, sliced
sea salt and black pepper to taste
4 eggs
4 cups romaine lettuce, chopped
3 cups mixed lettuce
1 cup cherry tomatoes, halved
1 cup red pepper, diced
1 cup Swiss cheese, cubed
2 avocados, sliced
bleu cheese crumbles

Mince, then mash the garlic to make a paste. In bowl, combine the garlic paste, mayonnaise, sour cream, parsley, dill, chives, Worcestershire sauce, salt, black pepper, vinegar, paprika, cayenne, and hot sauce. Whisk. Stir in cream to desired consistency. And seasonings as needed. Chill for one hour or more before serving. Thin with cream, if needed.

Cook the bacon in skillet over medium heat. Crumble in large pieces and set aside. Add the chicken and salt and pepper to the same pan with the bacon grease, and sauté over medium-high heat for approximately 4–6 minutes on each side (depending on their size) until done. Set aside. Boil eggs in water for 10–12 minutes. Place in bowl of cold water and peel. Cut eggs in quarters and set aside. In a large bowl, mix the lettuces, tomatoes, peppers, cheese, avocado, bacon bits, and eggs. Toss the salad with the dressing, and top with sliced chicken.

# Spirit

Most people do not listen with the intent to understand; they listen with the intent to reply.
—Stephen R. Covey

# * Cook

Invite friends over for dinner and cook, even if you don't think you're a great chef. Follow one of the recipes in this book—you can't go wrong. I love it so much when I am invited for dinner and love to reciprocate. I always find that the relaxed, intimate atmosphere of being in a home and sharing a meal allows for genuine quality time. We often will play a game afterward. This is a double-sided gift.

# Mind No. 23

What year was the first e-mail sent?

## Body

Classic Hummus
Serves 10–12 appetizer portions

2 cans chickpeas/garbanzo beans (15 ounces each), drained and
rinsed
1/3 cup tahini paste
8 roasted garlic cloves
2–5 jalapeños, seeded (optional, for a spicy version)
1/3 cup cilantro, chopped
1/4 cup fresh lemon juice, or more to taste
1 tablespoon extra-virgin olive oil
1 1/2 teaspoons cumin
3/4 teaspoons sea salt, to taste

Roast the garlic: preheat the oven to 400 degrees F. Peel the
outermost skin from the garlic head, leaving the cloves in their
casings. Slice off the top part of the garlic head, leaving the top of
cloves exposed. Drizzle with olive oil. Wrap the garlic in foil. Place
on small baking sheet. Cook for 45 minutes. Cool for several minutes
before unwrapping. Squeeze the cloves out from their casings.

Drain the chickpea water from one can into a small bowl and reserve. Put chickpeas, tahini paste, roasted garlic, seeded jalapeños (optional), chopped cilantro, lemon juice, olive oil, cumin, and salt into food processor or blender. (If using jalapeño peppers, heat levels tend to vary by pepper, so start with two; you can always add more to make it spicier.)

Pulse the ingredients for one minute; then process until smooth, scraping the sides of the processor occasionally. Taste the mixture and add more jalapeños, salt, or lemon juice to taste. Process again to blend any added ingredients. If the texture seems too thick, add some of the water from the chickpea can and continue to process until desired consistency.

## Spirit

Life is 10 percent of what happens to you and 90 percent of how you react to it.
—Charles R. Swindoll

## * Foreign City

Traveling anywhere foreign is an adrenaline rush for me. It is so exciting and exhilarating that I make it a point to go somewhere new every year. Perhaps it could be a city in the country where you live, or a city in a foreign country, or even a city thirty minutes away that you have never visited. New sights, sounds, and smells keep us aware, refreshed, and invigorated. Traveling really makes me happy.

# Mind No. 24

How many teeth does an African elephant have?

## Body

Basic Broccoli Slaw
Serves 4 (Paleo and gluten free)

1 12-ounce bag of shredded broccoli slaw (You can shred your own; if so, add some shredded carrot and red cabbage.)

Dressing
1/2 cup mayonnaise
1 1/4 teaspoons vinegar (I use balsamic)
2 teaspoons of sugar or 1 teaspoon of stevia
sea salt and cayenne pepper to taste

In large mixing bowl, blend together the dressing ingredients. Add slaw and toss.

## Spirit

As we express gratitude, we must never forget that the highest appreciation is not to utter words but to live by them.
—John F. Kennedy

# * Thank You So Much

It feels fabulous to receive a compliment. Let someone know you like his or her smile, hair, outfit, work performance, or eyes. I was recently in a shop, and my sales clerk said that I looked like one of my all-time favorite movie stars, Michelle Pfeiffer. It made my week, maybe my year. A simple compliment can make your spirit soar.

# Mind No. 25

In Greek mythology, who was the goddess of victory?

# Body

## Potato Corn Chowder
Serves 4

1 onion, chopped
2 cloves garlic, chopped
1 medium potato, cubed
2 celery stalks, sliced
1 small red pepper, seeded, halved, and sliced
2 tablespoons olive oil
2 tablespoons butter
2 1/2 cups of vegetable stock or chicken stock
1 1/4 cups milk
1 7-ounce can of pinto beans
3/4 cup of frozen or canned corn
pinch of Italian herbs
sea salt and cayenne or black cracked pepper to taste
shredded cheddar cheese

Place onion, garlic, potato, celery, and red pepper in large heavy pan with oil and butter. Heat until sizzling; then reduce to low. Cover and cook gently for 10 minutes, making sure ingredients don't stick.

Pour in stock, add salt and pepper, and bring to boil. Reduce heat, cover again, and simmer gently for 15 minutes until vegetables are tender. Add milk, beans with liquid, and corn. Simmer uncovered 5 minutes.

Garnish with shredded cheddar cheese.

## Spirit

The greatest weapon against stress is to choose one thought over another.
—William James

## * Mozart for the Mind

Many of us played a musical instrument growing up; maybe it was only the recorder. I took piano lessons for years, begrudgingly. I wish I had carried on with those lessons, but it is never too late to resume or begin to learn to play an instrument. Listening to classical music, especially Mozart, is also very inspirational. So if playing an instrument isn't for you, listen to the classics. Music is magically enticing to your spirit.

# Mind No. 26

How many months of the year have only thirty days?

# Body

## Super-Bowl Sunday Chili
Serves 8 (1 1/2 cup each)

3 tablespoons olive oil

1 large red onion, chopped (save some for garnish)

1 cup chopped red pepper

6 garlic cloves, minced

1 tablespoon cumin

1 tablespoon red pepper flakes or 1–2 jalapeno peppers, diced and seeded

6–8 tablespoons chili powder to taste (I sometimes add more)

1 carton (10 ounces) cherry tomatoes, halved

1 can (14.5 ounces) diced tomatoes

2 tablespoons tomato paste

2 cans (15 ounces each) pinto or chili beans, rinsed

1 can (15 ounces each) black beans, rinsed

1 1/2 cups chicken or beef broth (depends whether using turkey or beef)

1 tablespoon dry Italian herb seasonings

4 cups ground beef or turkey meat, cooked

1 tablespoon sea salt

1 pinch ground pepper
8 ounces cheddar cheese, shredded for garnish (optional)
1 cup sour cream for garnish (optional)

In a large soup pot over medium heat, heat olive oil. Add onion and peppers; stir until translucent. Add garlic, cumin, chili powder, and red pepper flakes, cooking for an additional 2 minutes. Add tomatoes (both fresh and canned), tomato paste, broth, rinsed beans, oregano, turkey or beef, and salt and pepper, and bring to a boil. Reduce heat to low, and simmer for an hour. Garnish chili with shredded cheese, sour cream, and chopped red onion.

# Spirit

Life is made of millions of moments, but we live only one of these moments at a time. As we begin to change this moment, we begin to change our lives.
—Trinidad Hunt

# * Love the Louvre

Visit a museum. Almost every city has a museum of some kind. Go visit your local one, or plan to visit one on your next travel adventure. Admiring great pieces of art, history, sculpture, furniture, fashion from history, or whatever the museum offers is so inspirational. I love antique furniture, clothing, paintings, sculptures, and Egyptian mummies. I recently visited Stonehenge, one of the greatest outdoor museums.

# Mind No. 27

What is the most common creature on earth?

# Body

## Very Berry Crumble
Serves 6–8

4 cups of fresh berries (blueberry, raspberry, strawberry, or blackberry, or a combination)
1/2 cup brown sugar
1 cup of flour
1 teaspoons baking powder
1 stick of butter plus 2 tablespoons
1 1/2 teaspoons tapioca
2 tablespoons white sugar
1 cup chopped pecans (optional)
whipped cream or ice cream

Lay berries in baking dish and sprinkle with white sugar and tapioca.

Combine brown sugar, flour, and baking powder. Chop in butter until mixture is like crumble; then sprinkle on top of the berries. Add chopped pecans, if desired. Bake at 350 degrees for 45 minutes. Serve warm with whipped cream or ice cream.

# Spirit

You always do what you want to do. This is true with every act. You may say that you had to do something, or that you were forced to, but actually, whatever you do, you do by choice. Only you have the power to choose for yourself.
—W. Clement Stone

## * Tick-Tock

Make it a point today to be on time. Growing up, I learned the hard way how important it was to be on time. If I missed curfew, I was grounded. As I matured, I realized that punctuality extends enormous respect to others. Also, it is self-gratifying to be accountable. We all know how inconvenient and worrisome it can be to wait. Give the gift of appreciating others' time.

# Mind No. 28

How many pairs of chromosomes does a human usually have?

# Body

## Asparagus with Hollandaise
Serves 4–6

3 egg yolks
2 tablespoons fresh lemon juice
1/2 cup of butter
dash of cayenne pepper
fresh asparagus, ends trimmed
1 tablespoon finely chopped large-leaf parsley (optional)

Steam asparagus in steamer on stovetop. While asparagus is streaming, put egg yolks, lemon juice, and cayenne pepper in blender. Blend for 5 seconds. Heat butter in a glass measuring cup in microwave. Turn blender on high speed, and pour butter through lid. Sauce should thicken slightly. Place the asparagus on a serving dish and pour the sauce over steamed asparagus immediately. Sprinkle with parsley.

# Spirit

The moment one definitely commits oneself, then Providence moves too. All sorts of things occur to help one that would never otherwise have occurred ... unforeseen incidents, meetings, and material assistance, which no man could have dreamed would have come his way.

—Johann Wolfgang von Goethe

# * Picasso

Take an art class, and express your inner creativity. Anyone can learn to draw or paint. I didn't think I could until I bought the book *Drawing on the Right Side of the Brain* by Betty Edwards. There is a companion video as well that teaches guided practices in the five basic skills of drawing. It is fun and challenging, and you can do it from home. I thought I could only draw stick figures, so I am very proud of myself with my sketches now—and you will be too.

# Mind No. 29

What is the world's most densely populated country?

# Body

## Catherine's Corn Bread
Serves 10

½ cup of granulated white sugar
1 egg
4 tablespoons of melted butter
1 cup of milk
1 cup of flour
1 cup of cornmeal
1 tablespoon of baking powder
½ teaspoon of salt
¼ cup of chopped fresh jalapeño peppers seeded (optional)

Heat the oven to 400 degrees. Spray the bottom and sides of an 8-inch square pan with the cooking spray. In a sauce pan, heat the butter over low heat until melted. In a large mixing bowl, beat the melted butter, milk and egg with a fork or a wire whisk until well mixed. Add the cornmeal, flour, sugar, baking powder and salt all at once; stir just until the flour is moistened (batter will be lumpy). Add the jalapeño peppers. (optional) Stir in slightly to mix. Pour batter into the pan; spread batter evenly and smooth the top of the batter, with a rubber spatula. Bake 20 to 25 minutes or until golden brown and a toothpick inserted in the center comes out clean. Serve warm.

# Spirit

Nowhere can man find a quieter or more untroubled retreat than in his own soul.
—Marcus Aurelius

# * Retirement

I love to hear people's stories, especially those who have been on the planet a long time. Visiting a retirement home and speaking with elderly people, to me, is a win/win situation. I especially like to visit during the holidays and bring a gift; it is always so appreciated. The joy and happiness you can bring is priceless.

# Mind No. 30

In Greek mythology, who fired the arrow that hit Achilles in the heel?

## Body

Gorgeous Ground Meat Tacos
Serves 6-8

1 pound of ground beef or turkey
hard or soft taco shells
2 tablespoons cooking oil
1 onion, chopped
2–3 cloves garlic, chopped
3 tablespoons chili powder
1/2 teaspoon cayenne pepper (more or less for spice)
2 teaspoons cumin
2 teaspoons coriander
2 tablespoons of broth, or as needed
1 cup shredded cheddar cheese
1/2 cup chopped tomatoes
1 cup shredded lettuce
sour cream
chopped cilantro (optional)

Sauté onion and garlic in oil. Add chili powder, cayenne pepper, cumin, and coriander. Cook 30 seconds. Add ground meat, and cook until browned. Add broth, and season to taste. Let simmer on low 10–15 minutes for flavor. Serve in hard or soft taco shells, and top with lettuce, tomatoes, cheese, and a dollop of sour cream (and cilantro, if desired).

# Spirit

Reflect upon your present blessings of which every man has plenty; not on your past misfortunes of which all men have some.
—Charles Dickens

# * Pumps

One of my favorite things to do is go shoe shopping. Treat yourself to a new pair of shoes. Even if a new pair of flip-flops is all the budget allows, getting them brings joy. I like to visit the outlet stores and find a great pair of shoes on sale. That really makes me happy.

# Mind No. 31

Who was known as the "Wizard of Menlo Park"?

# Body

Peter Piper's Pumpkin Pie
Serves 8-10

2 frozen 9-inch pie shells, thawed
1 16 ounce can pumpkin pie filling
4 eggs
1 cup sugar
1/2 cup brown sugar
2 teaspoons cinnamon
1/2 teaspoons ginger
1 teaspoons vanilla
dash nutmeg
dash cloves
2 cups half-and-half

Preheat oven to 425 degrees. Put pumpkin in a large mixing bowl. Add eggs, white and brown sugars, cinnamon, ginger, vanilla, nutmeg, and cloves. Beat until mixed. Slowly add half-and-half, and mix. Pour into shells. Place pies on baking sheet, and bake at 425 degrees for 15 minutes; then reduce to 350 degrees and bake for 45 more minutes or until toothpick comes out clean.

# Spirit

The greatest glory in living lies not in never falling but in rising every time we fall.
—Nelson Mandela

## * Movie, Anyone?

Watch a comedy or inspirational movie, or binge-watch a TV show. Take those thirty, sixty, ninety, or 120 minutes to laugh, cry, or be amazed. When I am having a down day, have too much going on, or can't make a decision, I love to transport myself into a great film and simply take my thoughts off everything. One of my all-time favorites is *Forrest Gump*. Answers seem to come easier, and life is *happy* when we allow ourselves simple pleasures. We can all learn a lot from Forrest.

# Mind No. 32

Which country has more lakes than all the other countries in the world combined?

## Body

Spicy Salsa with Cucumber or Corn Chips
Serves 6 (cucumber keeps it Paleo)

1 1/4 pounds tomatoes, finely chopped
2 diced avocadoes
1/2 cup finely chopped red onion
1/2 cup finely chopped cilantro
1–2 small jalapeño peppers, seeded and minced (depends on how spicy you want it)
2 tablespoons fresh lime juice
sea salt and freshly ground pepper
1 large cucumber, sliced 1/4 inch thick, or corn tortilla chips

In a bowl, toss the tomatoes, avocados, onion, cilantro, jalapeño, and lime juice, and season with salt and pepper. Serve with the cucumber and/or corn chips for dipping.

# Spirit

The appearance of things changes according to the emotions, and thus we see magic and beauty in them, while the magic and beauty are really in ourselves.
—Kahlil Gibran

## * Flowers

Flowers are a beautiful reminder of how magnificent Mother Nature is. Buy a bouquet for your home, or give a bouquet to someone. Don't wait for an occasion. The surprise and gratitude on the person's face will bring such joy to both of you. If you have space, be a gardener. Plant some flowers, or grow herbs or vegetables. It is gratifying to watch Mother Nature bloom.

# Mind No. 33

What language did Anne Frank use when she wrote her diary?

# Body

### Betty's Bread Pudding
Serves 6-8

6–8 slices day-old bread
2 tablespoons butter, melted
1/2 cup raisins (optional)
1/2 cup pecan pieces (optional)
4 eggs, beaten
2 cups milk
1/2 cup white sugar
1/4 cup brown sugar
1 teaspoon ground cinnamon
1 teaspoon vanilla extract

Preheat oven to 350 degrees F. In an 8-inch square baking pan, break bread into small pieces. Drizzle melted butter over bread. Sprinkle with raisins and pecans (optional). In a mixing bowl, combine eggs, milk, sugar, cinnamon, and vanilla. Beat until well mixed. Pour over bread, and gently push down with a fork until bread is covered and soaking up the egg mixture. Bake in the preheated oven for 45 minutes or until the top bounces back when gently tapped.

# Spirit

Happiness is not determined by what is happening around you, but rather what is happening inside you. Most people depend on others to gain happiness, but the truth is, it always comes from within.
— Unknown

## * Ethnic Restaurant

Go to an Indian, Thai, Chinese, Peruvian, Brazilian, or any ethnic restaurant that you have been reluctant to try or have been meaning to try. Expand your palette. I recently ate in a Peruvian restaurant in Chicago, and it was fabulous. I never would have thought to try Peruvian food. I loved it.

# Mind No. 34

Which is the only planet that rotates clockwise?

## Body

King Henry's British Meat Pie
Serves 6–8

2 pounds ground beef
1/2 large onion, chopped
2 tablespoons oil
1 1/2 tablespoons butter
3–5 garlic cloves, chopped
2 tablespoons seasoning salt
1 tablespoon garlic powder
1 teaspoon oregano
1/4 cup Worcestershire sauce
6 ounces beer (can substitute beef broth or 1 cup red wine)
3 cubes Oxo (beef bouillon)
1/4 cup heavy cream
pastry for a two-crust pie

Preheat oven to 425 degrees F. Sauté onions and garlic in oil and butter until golden. Add meat and brown lightly while adding Worcestershire, Oxo cubes, beer, cream, seasoning salt, garlic powder, and oregano. Simmer for 20 minutes. Spoon into deep pastry-lined 10-inch pie plate. Pat firm with spatula. Cover with top crust. Make a few slits in top. Brush pastry with milk. Bake for 30 minutes.

## Spirit

The trick is in what one emphasizes. We either make ourselves miserable, or we make ourselves happy. The amount of work is the same.
—Carlos Castaneda

## * Move Over

Be a giving driver, and move over when someone else is trying to merge onto the road. It is such a simple gesture, yet one that is kind and keeps the roads safe. I am so grateful when someone moves over for me. Let's make this one a daily practice.

# Mind No. 35

Which musician's real name is Robert Allen Zimmerman?

# Body

Easy-Peasy Lamb Chops
Serves 6 (Paleo and gluten free)

2–3 large garlic cloves, crushed
1 tablespoon fresh rosemary leaves
1 teaspoon fresh thyme leaves
1 tablespoon Italian herb seasoning
pinch cayenne pepper
coarse sea salt
2 tablespoons extra-virgin olive oil
6 lamb chops, about 3/4 inch thick

Finely chop the garlic, rosemary, and thyme. Add salt, cayenne, and Italian herb seasoning. Add olive oil. Rub mixture on both sides of the lamb chops, and let them marinate for 1 hour at room temp. Place on grill or pan on high heat. Sear for 2 minutes. Turn and cook another 3 minutes for medium rare, 3 ½ minutes for medium.

# Spirit

I have not failed. I have just found 10,000 ways that won't work.
—Thomas A. Edison

## * Underwater

Take a scuba diving course. What an adventure to journey to the underwater world. If that feels overwhelming—and I will admit it is for me—snorkeling is quite awesome too. I prefer to stay on top of the water, but all of those who do scuba dive, say it is the greatest, most wondrous activity they have ever experienced. There are PADI (Professional Association of Diving Instructors) locations in most cities. (See padi.com.)

# Mind No. 36

Who was King Henry VIII's first wife?

## Body

Charles's Chicken Pot Pie
Serves 16 (two pies 8 servings each) (pies can be frozen)

2 cups peeled and diced potatoes
1 3/4 cups diced carrots
1 cup butter, cubed
2/3 cup chopped onion
1 cup all-purpose flour
1 3/4 teaspoons sea salt
1 teaspoon dried thyme
3/4 teaspoon cayenne pepper
3 cups chicken broth
1 1/2 cups milk
4 cups cooked chicken, cubed
1 cup frozen peas
2 packages (14.1 ounces each) pie pastry

Preheat oven to 425 degrees. Put potatoes and carrots in saucepan; add water to cover. Bring to a boil. Reduce heat; cook covered until vegetables are al dente; drain. In a large skillet, melt butter over medium-high heat. Sauté onion until tender. Stir in flour and seasonings until blended. Gradually add broth and milk. Bring to a boil, stirring constantly. Stir 2 more minutes or until thickened. Add chicken, peas, carrots, and potatoes. Remove from heat.

Unroll a pastry sheet into each of two 9-inch pie plates; trim even with rims. Add chicken mixture. Unroll remaining pastry; place over filling. Trim and seal crusts together. Cut slits in tops. Brush with milk. Bake 35–40 minutes or until crust is lightly browned. Let stand 15 minutes before cutting.

## Spirit

The people who receive the most approval in life are the ones who care the least about it.
—Dr. Wayne Dyer

# * Lost in Translation

Learn a foreign language. I studied Spanish in high school and certainly know enough to get by in Spanish-speaking countries. My passion is French, though, and I have been learning the language for a while. I use Rosetta Stone for this tutoring and find it quite helpful. One day I will treat myself to a French immersion course to really master the language. It is awesome to be able to communicate in another language.

# Mind No. 37

How many sides does a snowflake have?

Body

## Terrific Turkey Burgers
Serves 4 ~6 ounce burgers (leave out the bread crumbs for Paleo and gluten-free)

1 1/2 pounds of ground turkey
1 cup feta cheese crumbles
1 tablespoon finely chopped rosemary
2–3 garlic gloves, finely chopped
1/2 cup finely chopped onion
sea salt
pinch cayenne pepper
2–3 tablespoons oil
1 egg (optional)
1/2 cup bread crumbs (optional)

Combine all ingredients in mixing bowl and mix well. Form 6 burger patties. Put oil in skillet or spray oil on both sides of each patty, for grilling. Place patties on surface, and cook 5 minutes each side or until desired doneness.

# Spirit

If you knew who walks beside you on this path that you have chosen, fear would be impossible. —*A Course in Miracles*

## * Give a Little More

What is a dollar here or there? A lot to someone else. If you normally tip your server 15 percent, give 20 percent; if you usually tip 20 percent, give 25 percent. You will make someone's day. When I was a struggling actress in New York City, working as a server, having a little extra money was cab or subway fare home on a cold snowy night, instead of walking twenty blocks. Perhaps your server is saving for a better education. Every penny counts, so give a little extra; it feels good. When you are in the checkout line at your local supermarket, and the clerk asks you to give to Feed the Hungry, give that dollar or five. It feels good.

# Mind No. 38

What is the most abundant element in the air we breathe?

# Body

## Shrimp with Chili and Lime
Serves 2 (Paleo and gluten-free)

12 large shrimp, peeled and deveined
2–3 tablespoons olive oil
juice of 2 limes
2 tablespoons honey or agave
1/4 teaspoon chili powder
1;4 teaspoon cayenne pepper
3 garlic cloves, chopped fine

In medium bowl, combine oil, lime juice, honey or agave, chili powder, and cayenne pepper. Add shrimp, and toss to coat. Refrigerate for 20–30 minutes.

In skillet, add olive oil and garlic, and sauté for 1–2 minutes. Add shrimp and sauté for 2–3 more minutes on each side or until pink. Serve immediately.

# Spirit

There are two days in the year that nothing can be done. One is called yesterday and the other is called tomorrow, so today is the right day to love, believe, do and mostly live.
—Dalai Lama

# * Master Chef

Take a cooking class. Williams-Sonoma and Sur La Table offer cooking classes. You can attend in person or take the class online. Attending in person is a blast. The classes at Sur La Table usually last about two to two and a half hours, and you cook in small groups of about four. They offer all kinds of classes, from desserts, to Indian cuisine, to grilling, to slicing. Some classes are complimentary, and others charge a minimal fee. Cooking makes me happy because it is creative and then yummy to eat.

# Mind No. 39

At what speed does light travel?

## Body

Beefy Beef Stew
Serves 4–6

1/4 cup flour, plus 1 tablespoon
2 teaspoons sea salt
1 teaspoon cayenne pepper
3 pounds beef stew-meat pieces
3 tablespoons olive oil
1 large onion chopped
2–3 cloves garlic, chopped
2 tablespoons tomato paste
1 cup dry red wine
4 cups (1 quart) beef broth
2 bay leaves
4 fresh thyme sprigs
3 whole carrots, sliced
3 whole celery stalks, sliced
4 medium russet potatoes (about 1 1/2 pounds), cubed
1 cup frozen peas

Put 1/4 cup of the flour, salt, and pepper in bowl and mix. Put meat in flour mixture and lightly coat; set aside. Heat oil in heavy-bottomed pot over medium heat. Shake off the excess flour from meat and add it to the pot. Cook until browned all over, about 4–5 minutes. (May need to be browned in batches.) Remove to large bowl. Repeat until all meat is browned; set aside. Add the onion and garlic to the pot, and season with more salt and pepper. Sauté until golden, about 5 minutes. Add tomato paste, coating onion, and cook about 1–2 minutes. Sprinkle in remaining tablespoon of flour, and cook, stirring occasionally, about 1 minute. Add in wine, scraping up any browned pieces, and cook until thickened, about 3 minutes. Return meat to the pot. Add broth, bay leaves, and thyme, and stir to combine. Turn heat to high and bring to a boil. Reduce heat and simmer uncovered for 1 hour. Add carrots, celery, and potatoes. Stir, cover, and simmer, stirring occasionally, until the vegetables and meat are tender, about 1 hour. Remove and discard the bay leaves and thyme stems. Add peas, and simmer uncovered about 5 minutes more. Season to taste.

## Spirit

It is the mark of an educated mind to be able to entertain a thought without accepting it.
—Aristotle

## * Join That Gym

Join that gym you keep talking about; just do it. Keeping your body healthy and strong is an anti-stress agent. Most gyms are very affordable now and offer a complimentary training session to help you get started. Gyms also offer great classes, such as spinning, yoga, boot camp, and Zumba. If weights are not your thing, there are so many other options at the gym now. You will be pleasantly surprised by how much more energy you will have. Dopamine, a neurotransmitter in the brain, is released when we exercise. Dopamine is necessary for feelings of pleasure and happiness. The more we work out, the happier we are.

# Mind No. 40

What is the name of William Shakespeare's longest play?

## Body

Simple Simon's Salmon
Serves 4

4 tablespoons soy sauce
1/2 cup honey
1–2 cloves garlic, minced
1/4 teaspoon garlic salt
1/4 teaspoon cayenne pepper
1 pound wild-caught salmon

In a small bowl, mix the honey, soy sauce, garlic, garlic salt, and pepper. Place salmon in a shallow glass baking dish, and coat with the honey-soy mixture. Cover the dish, and marinate salmon in the refrigerator 30 minutes, turning once. Preheat oven to 400 degrees F. Place the baking dish in the preheated oven, and bake salmon uncovered 20 minutes or until easily flakes with a fork.

## Spirit

An old Cherokee told his grandson, "My son, there is a battle between two wolves inside us all. One is evil. It is anger, jealousy,

greed, resentment, inferiority, lies, and ego. The other is good. It is joy, peace, love, hope, humility, kindness, empathy, and truth." The boy thought about it, and asked, "Grandfather, which wolf wins?" The old man quietly replied, "The one you feed."
—Author Unknown

# * Yoga

Take a yoga class; it is so good for your body. It lowers stress and improves your mood. Some yoga methods use specific meditation techniques to focus the mind on your breathing, which quiets the constant "mind chatter," allowing you to feel relaxed. Yoga can also boost oxygen levels to the brain, leaving you feeling happy and more content with everyday life.

# Mind No. 41

Who was known as the "Iron Lady"?

# Body

## Queen Margaret's Scottish Scotch Eggs
Serves 4

4 eggs, cooked and peeled
1 pound ground pork
2–3 cloves of garlic, minced
1/2 cup chopped onion
1 teaspoon chopped cilantro
1 teaspoon chopped thyme
1 teaspoon garlic powder
1 teaspoon paprika
3/4 cup of bread crumbs
1 egg beaten
flour
sea salt and cayenne pepper to taste

Preheat oven to 400 degrees F. In large bowl, mix pork and all seasoning with hands. Shape into four flat patties. Roll each cooked egg in flour to coat. Place egg on pork patty, and mold around egg. Dip patty into beaten egg, coat with bread crumbs entirely. Place on ungreased cookie sheet. Bake 35 minutes or until sausage is thoroughly cooked through.

# Spirit

If you have built castles in the air, your work need not be lost. That is where they should be. Now put the foundation under them.
—Henry David Thoreau

# * Walk

Take a thirty-minute walk. I am so grateful to live close to the beach. This is my Zen walking space. Wherever you live, find a path as close to nature as possible for your walk. Listen to the sound of the waves, hear the birds sing, feel the breeze, listen to the waterfall, smell the pine trees, breathe in the beauty, and still your thoughts to your immediate surroundings. For me, walking clears my self-talk and allows thoughtful insights of the universe to come forward. Some of my greatest inspirations have come forth when I have been on a walk.

# Mind No. 42

What is the most widely spoken language in the world?

## Body

Spaghetti Bolognese
Serves 4

1 ounce butter
1 tablespoons olive oil
1 carrot
2 stalks celery
1 onion
4 ounces bacon
1 pound ground beef
1 14-ounce can chopped tomatoes
2 bay leaves
sea salt
fresh ground black pepper or cayenne
2 cloves garlic, chopped
4 ounces mushrooms
½ cup of beef stock or 1 Oxo cube in 1/2 cup water
1 cup of red wine
2 tablespoons heavy cream
3/4 tablespoons tomato puree
thyme

oregano
Italian seasonings to taste

Slowly melt the butter and oil in a large pan, which can be covered.
Add chopped carrot, onion, celery, bacon, and bay leaves; simmer
until golden. Add ground beef and garlic; season well with salt,
pepper, and Italian seasonings. Cook until meat is no longer pink.
Add wine; cook until liquid reduces a little. Add mushrooms, thyme,
and oregano. Blend the tomato puree with the beef stock; then add
to pan along with the canned tomatoes. Stir well; then cover and
cook on lowest possible heat for a couple of hours.

Slow cooking is the key to this recipe to allow the flavors to meld.
As this dish slowly simmers, you will may need to add more liquid;
use either wine or a little water. After two hours or so, remove from
heat, remove bay leaves, add 2 tablespoons of cream, and stir well.

Serve with hot spaghetti, fresh baked garlic bread, and grated cheese.

## Spirit

Anyone can sympathize with the sufferings of a friend, but it
requires a very fine nature to sympathize with a friend's success.
—Oscar Wilde

## * Read a Book

Take the time to browse a book store. I love to get a coffee or
green tea and roam. I can spend a good hour choosing my next
adventure. For me, reading has always been a favorite gift to myself.
I love historical fiction; it is educational and exciting. I also like to
read at least a chapter every morning of an inspirational book. I
was given *Illusions* by Richard Bach when I was eighteen, and it set

my life on a course for which I am forever grateful. Look at the acknowledgments page of this book for suggestions for authors who write inspirational books; they are all brilliant. A chapter a day keeps the blues away. It always sets such a happy course for my day.

# Mind No. 43

What is the most common blood type?

# Body

## The Queen's Coronation Chicken Salad
Serves 4

2 skinless chicken breasts
1 tablespoon olive oil
3 tablespoons lemon juice
sea salt and freshly ground black pepper
pat of butter
1 shallot, finely chopped
2 teaspoons curry powder
2 tablespoons tomato purée
3 1/2 ounces dry white wine
3 1/2 ounces chicken stock
1 tablespoon orange marmalade
5 ounces mayonnaise
1 teaspoon cayenne pepper
1 ounce crème fraiche or sour cream
4 green onions, finely chopped
2 tablespoons coriander
1/2 cup raisins (optional)
Salad greens

Rub the olive oil all over the chicken. Scatter the lemon zest over chicken, and season with salt and black pepper. Place chicken in a steamer and then steam the chicken for 20–25 minutes, or until cooked through; then set aside to cool. Melt the butter in a frying pan. Add the shallot, and sauté for five minutes. Stir in the curry powder, and cook for 2–3 minutes. Stir in the tomato purée, and cook for another minute. Add the wine, and continue to cook until the volume of the liquid has reduced by half. Stir in the marmalade and stock; continue to simmer until the volume of the liquid has reduced by half. Set aside to cool. Mix the mayonnaise and the crème fraiche in a bowl until well combined; then stir in the curry dressing. Fold in the raisins, green onions, lemon juice, coriander, and cayenne pepper.

Cut the chicken into bite-sized pieces. Fold this into the mayonnaise mixture. Season with salt and freshly ground black pepper to taste. Serve over a bed of greens.

## Spirit

Ancient Egyptians believed that upon death they would be asked two questions and their answers would determine whether they could continue their journey in the afterlife. The first question was, "Did you bring joy?" The second was, "Did you find joy?'
—Leo Buscaglia

## * Meditate

I like to light a fragrant candle before I begin my meditation. It relaxes and centers me before beginning. I love listening to *Getting into the Vortex*, fifteen-minute guided meditations from Esther and Jerry Hicks (Abraham). There are so many great guided meditations available. I also love Dr. Brian Weiss's guided healing meditations,

Wayne Dyer's *ah* and *om* meditation, and Sonia Choquette's guided meditations, or I simply sit quietly and focus on good-feeling thoughts and positive intentions for five minutes. Morning is a great time for meditation, as it sets forth a powerful course for your day.

# Mind No. 44

In which US state was Microsoft founded?

# Body

## Must-Have Mac and Cheese
Serves 6

1 pound rigatoni pasta
1–2 tablespoons unsalted butter
1 tablespoon flour
2 1/2 cups milk
3/4 teaspoon sea salt
1/4 teaspoon black pepper
1 6-ounce package shredded mild or medium cheddar
1 6-ounce package shredded mozzarella
1 4-ounce package goat cheese
2 tablespoons grated Parmesan
1 6-ounce can of chopped green chilies, drained (optional)

Heat oven to 350 degrees. Coat 9 x 9 baking dish with nonstick cooking spray. Bring a large pot of salted water to a boil. Add pasta and cook 1 minute less than package directions. Drain. Heat butter in a medium saucepan over medium heat. Whisk in flour until smooth and beginning to bubble (about 1 minute). While whisking, add milk in a thin stream. Stir in salt and pepper and bring to a simmer. Cook, simmering and stirring, for 2 minutes. Toss 1/2 cup each of the cheddar and mozzarella in a bowl, set aside. Add remaining cheddar and mozzarella to sauce. Stir in goat cheese. Combine cheese sauce (and green chilies, if desired) with pasta, and stir to coat. Put into baking dish. Top with cheddar-mozzarella mixture, that was set aside, and Parmesan. Bake at 350 degrees for 20 minutes, until browned on top.

# Spirit

Every time you are tempted to react in the same old way, ask yourself if you want to be a prisoner of the past or a pioneer or the future.
—Deepak Chopra

# * Master Chef

Take a cooking class. Williams-Sonoma and Sur La Table offer cooking classes. You can attend in person or take the class online. Attending in person is a blast. The classes at Sur La Table usually last about two to two and a half hours, and you cook in small groups of about four. They offer all kinds of classes from desserts, to Indian cuisine, to grilling, to slicing. Some classes are complimentary, and others charge a minimal fee. Cooking makes me happy because it is creative and then yummy to eat.

# Mind No. 45

In which year were tobacco commercials banned from television networks?

# Body

## Cilantro-Ginger Flounder
Serves 4 (Paleo and gluten-free)

1 clove garlic, peeled
1/2 small jalapeño pepper
1 1/2-inch piece fresh ginger, peeled and roughly chopped
3 tablespoons freshly squeezed lime juice (about 2 limes)
1 cup loosely packed cilantro leaves
6 tablespoons olive oil
salt and seasoning to taste
freshly ground black pepper
4 flounder fillets (about 1 1/2 pounds), skin removed

Combine garlic, jalapeño pepper, ginger, lime juice, and cilantro in a blender. Remove the stopper from the blender, turn on the blender, and slowly drizzle in the olive oil. Process until the mixture is bright green and smooth. Season to taste with salt and black pepper.

Season both sides of the fillets with salt and black pepper. Brush each fillet with 1 tablespoon cilantro sauce. Fill a large, high-sided skillet with 1 inch of water. Bring to boil over high heat. Place a steamer basket in the skillet, and arrange the fillets in basket. Cover, and steam until the fish is just cooked through but still moist, about 5 to 6 minutes. Remove the fish from steamer, drizzle with additional cilantro sauce, and serve.

# Spirit

Respond to every call that excites your spirit.
—Rumi

# * Make Amends

Forgiveness is one of the most beneficial gifts you can give yourself. So make amends with anyone, you feel negativity towards, regardless of whether you are actually able to speak with the person or not. If you are unable to have a conversation, another excellent way to accomplish forgiveness is to write forgiving statements. In your journal or on a piece of paper, just write it out. It can be as simple as writing, "[insert name], I forgive you for all the things that have made me feel hurt, sad, or rejected. I also forgive myself for all the parts I have played in our relationship." I have found that repeatedly writing out the sentence, until I feel all negative feelings are released, is the best way to cleanse pent-up emotions and clear out old thought patterns.

# Mind No. 46

Copper and zinc combined make which alloy metal?

# Body

## Zappy Zucchini Bread
Makes 2 loaves

1 cup chopped unpeeled zucchini
2 eggs
1 cup of melted coconut oil
3 teaspoons vanilla
2 1/2 cups granulated sugar
3 cups flour
1 1/2 teaspoons baking powder
1 teaspoon baking soda
1 teaspoon salt
3 teaspoons cinnamon
1/2 cup chopped pecans

In a blender, add zucchini, eggs, oil, and vanilla, and mix. Pour mixture into a mixing bowl; add sugar. Sift in flour, baking powder, baking soda, salt, and cinnamon.

Add pecans. Should be consistency of cake batter.

Pour into greased and floured loaf pans, and bake at 325 degrees for 1 hour.

## Spirit

Many of life's failures are people who did not realize how close they were to success when they gave up.
—Thomas A. Edison

## * Grateful Eight

Make a list of eight things for which you are grateful. It could be anything. Some examples are:

- I'm grateful that I was on time for work today.
- I am grateful there was no traffic on my way to work.
- I am grateful for my car; it is my sanctuary where I listen to music while I travel.
- I am grateful for my house; it brings me a sense of peace and safety every time I enter it.
- I am grateful for my health and want to thank each cell in my body for doing its job seemingly effortlessly.
- I am so grateful for my friends and family; they are always there to listen to me and lend me support. I am grateful for being able to travel; it exhilarates my soul.
- I am grateful for my spouse; [his or her] smile always brightens my day.

You get the idea. Be sure to write the reasons why you are grateful. Writing the reasons boosts your vibration even higher, and you will feel gratitude more deeply.

# Mind No. 47

What is the only Central American country with English as its official language?

## Body

Paleo Pork Tenderloin
Serves 4 (Paleo and gluten free)

2 pounds pork tenderloin
1/4 cup Dijon mustard
2 tablespoons honey
2 tablespoons chopped fresh thyme (or dried Italian herbs)
2–3 garlic cloves, chopped fine
sea salt and cracked black pepper

Preheat oven to 375 degrees. Line a baking sheet with foil. Season the pork with salt and pepper; place on baking sheet. In small bowl mix together mustard, honey, garlic, and thyme. Spread mixture over top and sides of pork. Roast for 30 minutes or until cooked through. Let rest for 10 minutes, slice, and serve.

# Spirit

There is nothing that you can do that is worse for yourself, than to do something that you believe is inappropriate. And so, get clear and happy about whichever choice you make.
—Esther and Jerry Hicks (Abraham)

# * Ring, Ring

If you find yourself thinking about an old friend, make that connection; reach out to that person. I lost one of my closet college friends to cancer at age forty-seven. I had not seen her for over ten years and kept thinking about connecting with her. Unexpectedly, I was able to visit her on a trip to Washington, DC, a few months before her diagnosis. I am forever grateful that I made the time to visit and see her happy and full of life. Follow your intuition when a friend or relative pops into your head. Reach out to that person in the moment.

# Mind No. 48

How many people have walked on the moon?

# Body

Mama Mia Meatloaf
Serves 4–6

1 pound lean ground beef
1 pound ground turkey or pork
1 onion, chopped fine
1 carrot, chopped fine
1 celery stalk, chopped fine
2–3 garlic cloves, chopped fine
1 cup bread crumbs
2 large eggs
1/4 cup tomato paste
3 tablespoons dried Italian herbs
3 tablespoons Worcestershire sauce
sea salt and cayenne or black pepper to taste

Preheat oven to 350 degrees. In large bowl, combine and mix all ingredients well. Transfer to a loaf pan and shape. Bake for 1 hour. Remove and let stand 10 minutes. Slice and serve.

# Spirit

What lies before us and what lies behind us are small matters compared to what lies within us. And when we bring what is within out into the world, miracles happen.

—Henry David Thoreau

# * Tick Tock

Make it a point today to be on time. Growing up, I learned the hard way how important it was to be on time. If I missed curfew, I was grounded. As I matured, I realized that punctuality extends enormous respect to others. Also, it is self-gratifying to be accountable. We all know how inconvenient and worrisome it can be to wait. Give the gift of appreciating others' time.

# Mind No. 49

A rainbow consists of how many colors?

## Body

Artichoke-Spinach Dip
Serves 4–6 (Paleo, if served with crudité, and gluten free)

1 cup of finely chopped artichoke hearts
1/2 cup of finely chopped fresh spinach
1 cup of shredded Parmesan cheese
1 cup of mayonnaise

In mixing bowl, combine all ingredients. Preheat oven to 350 degrees. Spoon into shallow baking dish or pie plate, and bake for 30 minutes. Serve hot in the baking dish or transfer to another serving dish. Serve with crudité, crackers of choice, or both.

## Spirit

Remember—and this is very important—you're only one thought away from happiness, you're only one thought away from sadness. The secret lies in Thought. It's the missing link that everybody in this world is looking for … It's a gift that we were given to have the freedom to walk through life and see what we want to see. How much better than that can you get? That you have the freedom to walk through life and see as a free thinker, that is the greatest gifts ever, to be a free thinker.

—Sydney Banks

# * Dream Board

Create a dream board. Cut out pictures from magazines or print pictures from the Internet, and paste them on a white poster board. They could be pictures of things you would like to have, places you'd like to visit, a car you'd like to drive, a beautiful bouquet of flowers, the perfect job, jewelry you'd like, a relationship you'd like to be in, or your dream house. Fill your board with anything that you would love to have, be, or experience. I keep mine close to my desk, and every time I glance at it, a feeling of grateful expectation fills my being.

# Mind No. 50

Who was the first person in space?

## Body

Protein Bars
Makes 24 squares

1 cup butter (organic)
1 small jar of peanut or almond butter
1 cup honey
1 cup vanilla protein powder
6 cups quick oats (make sure to use quick oats)
2 cups nuts/seeds (I use pumpkin, sunflower, and coconut flakes)

Melt butter and honey. Add dry ingredients and mix together. Pour onto cookie sheet and roll out. Put in refrigerator to harden. Cut into squares.. Store in fridge. (Can be frozen.)

## Spirit

The greatest weapon against stress is our ability to choose one thought over another.
—William James

# * Thank You So Much

It feels fabulous to receive a compliment. Let someone know you like his or smile, hair, outfit, work performance, or eyes. I was recently in a shop, and my sales clerk said that I looked like one of my all-time favorite movie stars, Michelle Pfeiffer. It made my week, maybe my year. A simple compliment can make our spirits soar.

# Mind No. 51

Who said, "How wonderful it is that nobody need wait a single moment before starting to improve the world"?

## Body

Bacon-Wrapped Jalapeno Poppers
Serves 2–4

6 fresh jalapeno peppers, halved lengthwise and seeded
1 8-ounce package cream cheese or any cheese of your choice
12 slices of bacon

Preheat an outdoor grill or a broiler on high.
Spread or pack the cream cheese or cheese of choice into the jalapeno halves. Wrap with bacon, and secure with a toothpick. Place on grill or under broiler until bacon is crispy.

## Spirit

This too shall pass.
—Medieval Levant proverb

# * Play

Go play tennis, golf, racquet ball, or soccer, Dance around your living room, or take a dance class. Learn to tango. Go outside and shoot hoops, kick a ball, or go for a bike ride. Be a kid again. Play and be *happy*.

# Mind No. 52

How many legs does a scorpion have?

# Body

Sweet Potato Mash
Serves 4

2 large sweet potatoes, peeled and cut, to boil
1/2 cup half-and-half
4 tablespoons butter
2 tablespoons of honey
1/2 teaspoons of cinnamon

Boil the potatoes until tender; then drain in pan. Add all ingredients, and mix with an electric mixer until whipped to desired consistency.

# Spirit

The game of life is a game of boomerangs. Our thoughts, deeds and words return to us sooner or later with astounding accuracy.
—Florence Scovel Shinn

# * Salt Bath

Take a hot twenty-minute mineral salt bath. I love to soak in Dr. Teal's Epsom salts. My favorite is the lavender or the eucalyptus. Not only do the minerals relax and sooth the body, but I get the benefits of aromatherapy too. Pleasant aromas release serotonin, which is the brain's natural happy chemical. I buy Dr. Teal's Epsom salts in my local supermarket, and they are quite affordable. This is a great gift to give yourself before bed. Lighting a candle while soaking brings even more relaxation.

# The Simple Suggestions to nourish your Spirit

## 1. Walk

Take a thirty-minute walk. I am so grateful to live close to the beach. This is my Zen walking space. Wherever you live, find a path as close to nature as possible for your walk. Listen to the sound of the waves, hear the birds sing, feel the breeze, listen to the waterfall, smell the pine trees, breathe in the beauty, and still your thoughts to your immediate surroundings. For me, walking clears my self-talk and allows thoughtful insights of the universe to come forward. Some of my greatest inspirations have come forth when I have been on a walk.

## 2. Meditate

I like to light a fragrant candle before I begin my meditation. It relaxes and centers me before beginning. I love listening to *Getting into the Vortex*, fifteen-minute guided meditations from Esther and Jerry Hicks (Abraham). There are so many great guided meditations available. I also love Dr. Brian Weiss's guided healing meditations, Wayne Dyer's *ah* and *om* meditation, and Sonia Choquette's guided meditations, or I simply sit quietly and focus on good-feeling thoughts and positive intentions for five minutes. Morning is a great time for meditation, as it sets forth a powerful course for your day.

## 3. Ring, Ring

If you find yourself thinking about an old friend, make that connection; reach out to that person. I lost one of my closet college friends to cancer at age forty-seven. I had not seen her for over ten years and kept thinking about connecting with her. Unexpectedly, I was able to visit her on a trip to Washington, DC, a few months before her diagnosis. I am forever grateful that I made the time to visit and see her happy and full of life. Follow your intuition when a friend or relative pops into your head. Reach out to that person in the moment.

## 4. Give a Little More

What is a dollar here or there? A lot to someone else. If you normally tip your server 15 percent, give 20 percent, If you usually tip 20 percent, give 25 percent. You will make someone's day. When I was a struggling actress in New York City, working as a server, having a little extra money was cab or subway fare home on a cold snowy night, instead of walking twenty blocks. Perhaps your server is saving for a better education. Every penny counts, so give a little extra; it feels good. When you are in the checkout line at your local supermarket, and the clerk asks you to give to Feed the Hungry, give that dollar or five. It feels good.

## 5. Pay That Toll

Surprise the car behind you on the toll way, and pay its toll. It may be a blessing in disguise for that person. A friend of mine lost her father unexpectedly and was grieving. She was asking for a sign that her father was still near and that he knew how much she loved him. She received her sign while driving through a toll booth. While handing her fare to the toll booth operator, he said, "The car in front already paid for you." It was the same random act of kindness her father always did. She knew then that her father was close and that all was well. It comforted her greatly.

## 6. Salt Bath

Take a hot twenty-minute mineral salt bath. I love to soak in Dr. Teal's Epsom salts. My favorite is the lavender or the eucalyptus. Not only do the minerals relax and sooth the body, but we get the benefits of aromatherapy too. Pleasant aromas release serotonin, which is the brain's natural happy chemical. I buy Dr. Teal's Epsom salts in my local supermarket, and they are quite affordable. This is a great gift to give yourself before bed. Lighting a candle while soaking brings even more relaxation.

## 7. Make Amends

Forgiveness is one of the most beneficial gifts you can give yourself. So make amends with anyone, you feel negativity towards, regardless of whether you are actually able to speak with the person or not. If you are unable to have a conversation, another excellent way to accomplish forgiveness is to write forgiving statements. In your journal or on a piece of paper, just write it out. It can be as simple as writing, "[insert name], I forgive you for all the things that have made me feel hurt, sad, or rejected. I also forgive myself for all the parts I have played in our relationship." I have found that repeatedly writing out the sentence, until I feel all negative feelings are released, is the best way to cleanse pent-up emotions and clear out old thought patterns.

# 8. Movie, Anyone?

Watch a comedy or inspirational movie, or binge-watch a TV show. Take those 30, 60, 90, or 120 minutes to laugh, cry, or be amazed. When I'm having a down day, have too much going on, or can't make a decision, I love to transport myself into a great film and simply take my thoughts off everything. One of my all-time favorites is *Forrest Gump*. Answers seem to come easier and life is happy when we allow ourselves simple pleasures. We can all learn a lot from Forrest.

# 9. Thank You So Much

It feels fabulous to receive a compliment. Let someone know you like his or her smile, hair, outfit, work performance, or eyes. I was recently in a shop, and my sales clerk said that I looked like one of my all-time favorite movie stars, Michelle Pfeiffer. It made my week, maybe my year. A simple compliment can make our spirits soar.

# 10. Grateful Eight

Make a list of eight things for which you are grateful. It could be anything. Some examples are:
- I'm grateful that I was on time for work today.
- I am grateful there was no traffic on my way to work.
- I am grateful for my car; it is my sanctuary where I listen to music while I travel.
- I am grateful for my house; it brings me a sense of peace and safety every time I enter it.
- I am grateful for my health and want to thank each cell in my body for doing its job seemingly effortlessly.

- I am so grateful for my friends and family; they are always there to listen to me and lend me support.
- I am grateful for being able to travel; it exhilarates my soul.
- I am grateful for my spouse; (his or her) smile always brightens my day.

You get the idea. Be sure to write the reasons why you are grateful. Writing the reasons boosts your vibration even higher, and you will feel gratitude more deeply.

## 11. Dream Board

Create a dream board. Cut out pictures from magazines or print pictures from the Internet, and paste them on a white poster board. They could be pictures of things you would like to have, places you'd like to visit, a car you'd like to drive, a beautiful bouquet of flowers, the perfect job, jewelry you'd like, a relationship you'd like to be in, or your dream house. Fill your board with anything that you would love to have, be, or experience. I keep mine close to my desk, and every time I glance at it, a feeling of grateful expectation fills my being.

## 12. Spring Clean

Clean out your closet. It doesn't have to be spring; let it be winter, summer, or fall as well. When we clear out the old, it makes room for the new—cliché but true. I love shopping, so clearing out leaves room to fill the hole I just created. This is a double-sided gift. Give your gently worn items to someone who has a hole in his or her closet. It could be a friend, coworker, employee, the Red Cross, Goodwill, the Salvation Army, or anyone in need. I have a few friends whose "gently worn" clothes I would love to have. You could also sell them or consign them and earn a little money. That always makes me happy.

## 13. Yoga

Take a yoga class. It is so good for your body. It lowers stress and improves your mood. Some yoga methods use specific meditation techniques to focus the mind on your breathing, which quiets the constant "mind chatter," allowing you to feel relaxed. Yoga can also boost oxygen levels to the brain, leaving you feeling happy and more content with everyday life.

## 14. Read a Book

Take the time to browse a bookstore. I love to get a coffee or green tea and roam. I can spend a good hour choosing my next adventure. For me, reading has always been a favorite gift to myself. I love historical fiction; it is educational and exciting. I also like to read at least a chapter every morning of an inspirational book. I was given *Illusions* by Richard Bach when I was eighteen, and it set my life on a course for which I am forever grateful. Look at the acknowledgments page of this book for suggestions of authors who write inspirational books; they are all brilliant. A chapter a day keeps the blues away. It always sets such a happy course for my day.

## 15. Be of Service

Donate your time. I have friends who rescue animals weekly from shelters. Serve a meal at a homeless shelter, even if it's a once-a-year Thanksgiving dinner. A dear friend of mine donates her time to prison inmates. She spends entire weekends in the prison, uplifting the inmates' spirits by sharing her loving wisdom and guiding them to see their self-worth. A remarkable way to be truly grateful for what we have, each and every day, is by giving to others.

## 16. Cook

Invite friends over for dinner and cook, even if you don't think you're a great chef. Follow one of the recipes in this book—you can't go wrong. I love it so much when I am invited for dinner and love to reciprocate. I always find that the relaxed, intimate atmosphere of being in a home and sharing a meal allows for genuine quality time. We often will play a game afterward. This is a double-sided gift.

## 17. Move Over

Be a giving driver, and move over when someone else is trying to merge onto the road. It is such a simple gesture, yet one that is kind and keeps the roads safe. I am so grateful when someone moves over for me. Let's make this one a daily practice.

## 18. Flowers

Flowers are a beautiful reminder of how magnificent Mother Nature is. Buy a bouquet for your home, or give a bouquet to someone. Don't wait for an occasion. The surprise and gratitude on the person's face will bring such joy to both of you. If you have space, be a gardener. Plant some flowers, or grow herbs or vegetables. It is gratifying to watch Mother Nature bloom.

## 19. Play

Go play tennis, golf, racquet ball, or soccer. Dance around your living room, or take a dance class. Learn to tango. Go outside and shoot hoops, kick a ball, or go for a bike ride. Be a kid again. Play and be happy.

## 20. Tick-Tock

Make it a point today to be on time. Growing up, I learned the hard way how important it was to be on time. If I missed curfew, I was grounded. As I matured, I realized that punctuality extends enormous respect to others. Also, it is self-gratifying to be accountable. We all know how inconvenient and worrisome it can be to wait. Give the gift of appreciating others' time.

## 21. Mani-Pedi

Schedule an appointment for a manicure and/or pedicure. You deserve it. I don't always have time for both, but I certainly make it a point to have one or the other. It's relaxing, calming, and refreshing. Invite a friend. Perhaps go for a meal afterward, and celebrate your beautiful new nails. Guys, this is for you too. I know many men who love to get mani-pedis. If you haven't tried it, don't be afraid. Now is the time.

## 22. Join That Gym

Join that gym you keep talking about; just do it. Keeping your body healthy and strong is an anti-stress agent. Most gyms are very affordable now and offer a complimentary training session to help you get started. Gyms also offer great classes, such as spinning, yoga, boot camp, and Zumba. If weights are not your thing, there are so many other options at the gym now. You will be pleasantly surprised by how much more energy you will have. Dopamine, a neurotransmitter in the brain, is released when we exercise. Dopamine is necessary for feelings of pleasure and happiness. The more we work out, the happier we are.

## 23. Ethnic Restaurant

Go to an Indian, Thai, Chinese, Peruvian, Brazilian, or any ethnic restaurant that you have been reluctant to try or have been meaning to try. Expand your palette. I recently ate in a Peruvian restaurant in Chicago, and it was fabulous. I never would have thought to try Peruvian food. I loved it.

## 24. Mozart for the Mind

Many of us played an instrument growing up; maybe it was only the recorder. I took piano lessons for years, begrudgingly. I wish I had carried on with those lessons, but it is never too late to resume or begin to learn to play an instrument. Listening to classical music, especially Mozart, is also very inspirational. If playing an instrument isn't for you, listen to the classics. Music is magically enticing to your spirit.

## 25. Foreign City

Traveling anywhere foreign is an adrenaline rush for me. It is so exciting and exhilarating that I make it a point to go somewhere new every year. Perhaps it could be a city in the country where you live, or a city in a foreign country, or even a city thirty minutes away that you have never visited. New sights, sounds, and smells keep us aware, refreshed, and invigorated. Traveling really makes me happy.

## 26. Retirement

I love to hear people's stories, especially those who have been on the planet a long time. Visiting a retirement home and speaking with elderly people, to me, is a win/win situation. I especially like to visit during the holidays and bring a gift. It is always so appreciated. The joy and happiness you can bring is priceless.

## 27. Rock and Roll

I had forgotten how awesome it is to attend a concert. What an extraordinary sensation it is to hear live music you love. I recently saw U2, one of my all-time favorite bands. I had not seen them in a decade and was walking on cloud nine for days. So many of their songs bring back fabulous memories and good-feeling thoughts.

## 28. Theatre or Comedy

Go see a theatrical production or a comedy show. It doesn't have to be Broadway or the West End. Most cities and towns have local theater—attend! If comedy is your thing, go to a comedy club, and laugh, laugh, laugh. Either experience is vitalizing.

## 29. Stay-cation

Occasionally, I like to just stay home and do nothing. Do whatever your *nothing* is—binge-watch a TV series, bake a cake, or lie in bed all day. I like to use the term "stay-cation"—it's a vacation while staying home. Invite friends to stay for the weekend and lounge around. playing games and laughing.

## 30. Mirror, Mirror on the Wall

Look in the mirror and tell yourself how loved and appreciated you are at least eight times out loud or until you really mean it. Yes, it can feel awkward at first, but it's a great exercise. I learned this exercise from Louise Hay. She offers so many self-love activities. Explore more at Hayhouse.com. It all begins with the love of ourselves.

## 31. Picasso

Take an art class, and express your inner creativity. Anyone can learn to draw or paint. I didn't think I could until I bought the book *Drawing on the Right Side of the Brain* by Betty Edwards. There is a companion video as well that teaches guided practices in the five basic skills of drawing. It is fun and challenging, and you can do it from home. I thought I could only draw stick figures, so I am very proud of myself with my sketches now—and you will be too.

## 32. Love the Louvre

Visit a museum. Almost every city has a museum of some kind. Go visit your local one, or plan to visit one on your next travel adventure. Admiring great pieces of art, history, sculpture, furniture, fashion from history, or whatever the museum offers is so inspirational. I love antique furniture, clothing, paintings, sculptures, and Egyptian mummies. I recently visited Stonehenge, one of the greatest outdoor museums.

## 33. Underwater

Take a scuba diving course. What an adventure to journey to the underwater world. If that feels overwhelming—and I will admit it is for me—snorkeling is quite awesome too. I prefer to stay on top of the water, but all of those who do scuba dive, say it is the greatest, most wondrous activity they have ever experienced. There are PADI (Professional Association of Diving Instructors) locations in most cities. (See padi.com.)

## 34. Pumps

One of my favorite things to do is go shoe shopping. Treat yourself to a new pair of shoes. Even if a new pair of flip-flops is all the budget allows, it brings joy. I like to visit the outlet stores and find a great pair of shoes on sale. That really makes me happy.

## 35. Master Chef

Take a cooking class. Williams-Sonoma and Sur La Table offer cooking classes. You can attend in person or take the class online. Attending in person is a blast. The classes at Sur La Table usually last about two to two and a half hours, and you cook in small groups of about four. They offer all kinds of classes from desserts, to Indian cuisine, to grilling, to slicing. Some classes are complimentary, and others charge a minimal fee. Cooking makes me happy because it is creative and then yummy to eat.

## 36. Facial

Give your face a present and have a facial. Facial treatments feel good, offering soothing relaxation. They increase circulation and blood flow, relieve stress, and encourage peace of mind and contentment. A good facial (and facial massage) can help smooth fine lines and promote collagen production, which is the building block of the skin, to prevent premature aging, wrinkles, and sagging. Facials are fabulous.

## 37. Massage

Treat yourself to a massage. Some studies have found massage may be beneficial for anxiety, digestive disorders, fibromyalgia, headaches, insomnia related to stress, soft-tissue strains or injuries, and sports injuries. Massages are now so affordable, with places like Hand and Stone Spa and Massage Envy club memberships. I treat myself to a massage at least once a month—and you should too.

# 38. Lost in Translation

Learn a foreign language. I studied Spanish in high school and certainly know enough to get by in Spanish-speaking countries. My passion is French, though, and I have been learning the language for a while. I use Rosetta Stone for this tutoring and find it quite helpful. One day I will treat myself to a French immersion course to really master the language. It is awesome to be able to communicate in another language.

# The Mind Answers

1. Venus
2. One
3. Wabash, Indiana
4. Columbia University
5. Jawbone
6. Tooth enamel
7. 1961
8. Four
9. Fifty-six
10. Hydrogen
11. -40 degrees
12. *The Great Gatsby*
13. Canada
14. 24,901
15. Mount Vesuvius
16. Bone marrow
17. Parliament
18. Twenty-seven
19. Rome, Italy
20. Liver
21. Radio Detection and Ranging
22. Limestone
23. 1971
24. Four
25. Nike
26. Four

27. Beetle
28. Twenty-three
29. Monaco
30. Paris
31. Thomas Edison
32. Canada
33. Dutch
34. Venus
35. Bob Dylan
36. Catherine of Aragon
37. Six
38. Nitrogen
39. 186,000 miles per second
40. *Hamlet*
41. Margaret Thatcher
42. Chinese Mandarin
43. O-positive
44. New Mexico
45. 1971
46. Brass
47. Belize
48. Twelve
49. Seven
50. Yuri Gagarin
51. Anne Frank
52. Eight

# About the Author

Elizabeth Baldwin-Lodge is an actress, interior designer, personal motivator, and family proclaimed fabulous home chef. Elizabeth's television and film credits include *Days of Our Lives, The Hogan Family, The Bold and the Beautiful, Mike Hammer Private Eye*, and *Watercolor Postcards*, to name a few. Elizabeth also designs residential interiors and was voted one of the Design Minds of the Year in 2010. She has received several other design awards of distinction. Elizabeth Baldwin-Lodge received her bachelor of arts degree in communications and theater arts from Pepperdine University, Malibu, California.

From a young age, Elizabeth has been inspired to travel a road of self-discovery, hoping to bring more happiness to the world. She hopes to be an inspiration and motivating force to all those she comes across.

www.elizabethbaldwin-lodge.com

Printed in the United States
By Bookmasters